PET
PRACTICE
— TESTS —

Five tests for the
Cambridge Preliminary
English Test

• DIANA L FRIED-BOOTH •

WITH ANSWERS

OXFORD UNIVERSITY PRESS

Oxford University Press
Great Clarendon Street, Oxford OX2 6DP

Oxford New York
Athens Auckland Bangkok Bogotá Buenos Aires
Cape Town Chennai Dar es Salaam Delhi Florence
Hong Kong Istanbul Karachi Kolkata Kuala Lumpur
Madrid Melbourne Mexico City Mumbai Nairobi
Paris São Paulo Shanghai Singapore Taipei
Tokyo Toronto Warsaw

and associated companies in
Berlin Ibadan

OXFORD and OXFORD ENGLISH
are trade marks of Oxford University Press

ISBN 0 19 453444 8

© Oxford University Press 1996

First published 1996
Third impression 2001

Typeset by Oxford University Press

Printed in China

Acknowledgements

The author and publisher would like to thank the following
for permission to use extracts and adaptations of
copyright material in this book:

AA Foundation for Road Safety Research: 'Accident risk
and behavioural patterns of younger drivers' (1991), study
undertaken by the Transportation Research Group and the
Department of Psychology at the University of
Southampton.

Biss Lancaster plc: information leaflet produced by the
Steel Can Recycling Information Bureau.
Europa Park: logo
Gatwick Express Ltd: information brochure.
Department of Health: booklet T5 – *Health Advice for
Travellers*.
Griffith Observatory: public information brochure.
South-Eastern International, British Railways: Euro-Youth
rail ticket leaflet.

Despite every effort to contact copyright holders before
publication this has not always been possible. If notified
the publishers will be pleased to rectify any errors or
omissions at the earliest opportunity.

The tests were piloted with various schools and groups of
students but the author is especially indebted to the
following teachers for their help: Alicia Balsells, Phyllis
Vannuffel, Susan Garvin, Matthew Hancock and Mark
Stone. The author is also grateful to the students from
various schools who have allowed their work to be used in
providing sample answers, in particular students from The
William Blake School in Buenos Aires, ITS School of
English in Hastings, the Swan School in Oxford and Wells
Cathedral School in Somerset.

The author is grateful to the University of Cambridge Local
Examinations Syndicate for permission to reproduce the
sample answer sheets on pages 106–109 and the
information on pages 113 and 128 in the With Answers
edition.

The author and publishers are especially grateful to
Howard Fried-Booth for supplying the photographs for the
Speaking Sections in the book.

The publisher would also like to thank Gatwick Express
Limited and Debra Emmett for their permission to
reproduce photographs.

Illustrations by Oxford Illustrators Limited

Commissioned photography by Rob Judges

Signs by P Squared Design

CONTENTS

INTRODUCTION

This book contains five complete practice tests for the Cambridge Preliminary English Test (PET), revised in 1996. Although the revised PET is broadly the same as the original test, the tests in this book reflect the changes in format and also incorporate the topic and vocabulary recommendations from the Threshold Level 1990. At this level, learners are expected to cope with the language of everyday situations for general purposes. This means that a learner, in the role of a tourist, for example, should be able to deal with the kind of language she or he will come across in the course of their daily travels. This would entail reading relevant travel documents, asking for help at a tourist office, booking accommodation, dealing with any problems, filling in forms or applications, writing short and simple letters – in other words being able to participate in everyday life without needing to resort to any specialized language.

Candidates have to write their answers on special answer sheets, OMRs (Optical Mark Readers) for Paper 1 (Reading and Writing) and Paper 2 (Listening). In Part 3 of the Writing paper, although candidates can write their answers on the question paper the written task must be transferred to the OMR sheet within the time allowed. At the end of the Listening Test, extra time is allowed for candidates to transfer their answers onto the OMR sheets. See pages 106-109 for examples of these answer sheets.

PAPER 1
READING AND WRITING TEST

(1 hour 30 minutes)

Reading

This paper has five parts with a total of 35 questions based on a variety of reading texts and tasks. As far as possible, the material is based on authentic sources such as newspapers, magazines, brochures, leaflets, advertisements, etc. which may have to be adapted or edited to keep within the linguistic framework of PET.

Part 1 consists of five short multiple-choice questions based on signs, notices and advertisements.

Part 2 consists of matching five short descriptions of individual people or groups of people to eight short texts; three texts are not used.

Part 3 is a single text with 10 true/false questions which require candidates to select specific information from the text.

Part 4 is an extract from a continuous text with five multiple-choice questions, which test understanding of opinion and attitude as well as specific information.

Part 5 is a gapped text with 10 multiple-choice questions designed to test understanding of vocabulary and grammatical structure.

Writing

This paper has three parts with a total of 16 questions.

Part 1 has five sentences which are all related to one theme. Candidates have to rewrite each sentence keeping the same meaning but using a different structural pattern from the original sentence. The beginning of each new sentence is provided.

Part 2 is a form with 10 questions which candidates must fill in with basic personal information, e.g. name, address and nationality using a number of words.

Part 2 has changed. (from 2004). Now a short text.

Part 3 requires a short text, about 100 words, usually in the form of a letter and always in an informal style. The task is based on information given at the beginning of the question and the opening sentence is provided.

PAPER 2
LISTENING TEST

(approximately 30 minutes + 12 minutes to transfer answers)

This paper has four parts with a total of 25 questions based on recorded material which candidates hear twice.

Part 1 consists of seven short dialogues or occasionally statements preceded by a question. Each recording is *Part 1 — 3 pictures (from 2004).* as they listen.

Part 2 is a recording, often of a simulated radio programme with six multiple-choice questions which test understanding of factual information.

Part 3 consists of a recording with six gapped questions which candidates complete using a number or a few words. It tests their ability to select relevant information.

Part 4 is a recorded dialogue between two people with six yes/no questions. Candidates are tested in their understanding of the speakers' differences in opinions and feelings.

SPEAKING TEST

(10–12 minutes)

This test is taken by candidates in pairs with two examiners, one of whom also acts as the interlocutor, i.e. gives the candidates their instructions and asks the questions. It may be necessary to examine candidates in a group of three at the end of a testing session if there is an odd number of candidates. The test is divided into four parts, and each part takes two to three minutes. The test will last slightly longer for groups of three candidates.

Part 1 consists of a general conversation in which the candidates find out personal information about each other, e.g. name, nationality, family background.

Part 2 is a situation, usually based on visual material, which the candidates discuss with each other, e.g. organizing a day trip.

Part 3 is based on a topic. Each candidate is given a different photograph, which they describe individually before comparing both photographs together.

Part 4 develops directly from the topic in Part 3, and gives candidates an opportunity to express their own personal opinions and attitudes in response to the examiner's questions.

MARKING

Each paper in PET is worth 25% of the total mark. In the Reading paper, however, as the raw (actual) score comes to 35 marks, the score is weighted to 25%.

A pass mark at PET is approximately 70%. Candidates are issued with individual result slips stating whether they have passed with merit, passed, narrowly failed or failed. Successful candidates are awarded a certificate.

For further information about the PET, write to:

EFL Section
University of Cambridge Local Examinations Syndicate
1 Hills Road
Cambridge CB1 2EU
UK

[The use of colour backgrounds to texts may differ from UCLES' own use.]

PAPER 1
Reading and Writing Test

(1 hour 30 minutes)

Reading

Part 1

Questions 1–5

● Look at the sign in each question.
● Someone asks you what it means.
● Mark the letter next to the correct explanation – **A**, **B**, **C** or **D** – **on your answer sheet.**

Example:

0

A Come in whenever you like.

B Please ring for an appointment.

C We will call you when we are free.

D Visitors please wait outside.

Example answer:

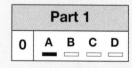

1

A Please do not take these seats.

B These seats are already reserved.

C Stay here if you want a seat.

D These seats are not being used.

2

A   Leave this gate open during the day.

B   This gate must never be left open.

C   There is no lock on this gate.

D   Please close this gate carefully.

3

A   Each tour lasts less than two hours.

B   A tour leaves here every two hours.

C   The tour is longer than two hours.

D   Each tour is under an hour long.

4

A   You cannot buy a drink until the interval.

B   Drinks are served here before the interval.

C   You can ask for drinks in time for the interval.

D   Drinks are served just after the start of the interval.

5

A   Villagers take care of these gardens.

B   These gardens are privately owned.

C   We are looking for a new gardener.

D   Visitors may not use these gardens.

[Turn over

Part 2

Questions 6–10

- The people below all want to book a day out by train.
- On the opposite page there are descriptions of eight day trips.
- Decide which trip (**letters A–H**) would be the most suitable for each person (**numbers 6–10**).
- For each of these numbers mark the correct letter **on your answer sheet**.

Example answer:

Part 2								
0	A	B	C	D	E	F	G	H
	▬	▭	▭	▭	▭	▭	▭	▭

6

Mrs Williams and her friend enjoy visiting old buildings especially in large city centres, but they are not free on a Saturday as they have to work.

7

Jean-Paul loves the countryside and is keen on taking photographs, so he is looking for a trip which will give him both possibilities.

8

Jancis and Tony would like a trip to the country that does not leave London before nine o'clock as they hate getting up early.

9

Sarah and her brother love eating on a train and want a trip that includes three meals. They are on holiday in June and would also like to visit a museum.

10

Tim is looking for a Saturday trip but he must be back in London by 21.00 hours so that he can catch the last bus home. He is interested in boats and sailing.

A

SUNDAY 20 OCTOBER

Lovely Somerset in Autumn! Leave London about 8.30, call at Reading with breakfast served as we head for Weston-super-Mare. Transfer to coaches for a road tour of the beautiful countryside before our first stop in Wells. Board the train again at Taunton for the journey home during which dinner will be served. Arrive London about 21.00 hours.

B

SATURDAYS 17 & 24 AUGUST

Visit the splendid Summer Festival in Malvern these two weekends. Special trains leave London about 8.15 and call at Reading as breakfast is served. Travel out to Wales and enjoy lunch before arrival in Malvern. Now there is time to visit the Festival before catching the train for the homeward journey. Dinner will be served and we will arrive in London at 21.30.

C

SATURDAY 1 JUNE

Train leaves London 07.00 and breakfast is served as we head north. Arrive Durham after a light lunch and visit this city full of history with its famous castle and cathedral. Travel by coach to the open-air Museum of Northern Life just outside Durham. Leave Durham station for the journey home arriving in London after dinner on board at 22.00 hours.

D

SUNDAY 23 JUNE

Try a Sunday luxury day out! Train leaves London about 9.00 and breakfast is served on the journey. Transfer to a comfortable coach at Repford station which takes you straight to the famous Shockton House built in the heart of the city in the sixteenth century. Arrive back in London at 21.30 hours.

E

SATURDAYS 15 JUNE AND 31 AUGUST

New route for 1997. Train leaves London about 08.30. Breakfast and a light lunch will be served on the journey and the train will run slowly over the most beautiful parts of the route. Leave the train in the Lake District and take the opportunity to photograph the countryside. Dinner will be served during the journey back, arriving in London at 21.30 hours.

F

SUNDAY 9 JUNE

This trip is especially for photographers. Leaving London at 09.30 for the Museum of Photography in the west country. Lunch is served on arrival at the Museum and after a short talk by the Museum Director you are free to enjoy the exhibitions in the afternoon. Train arrives back in London at 20.00 hours.

G

SATURDAY 8 JUNE

Train leaves London about 09.15 with breakfast served on the way. At Chepstow we transfer to coaches and drive to the lovely Wye Valley where there will a boat waiting to take you on a river trip. We will stop on the way for a short walk. Dinner will be served on the return trip, arriving back in London at 21.30 hours.

H

SATURDAY 22 JUNE

A day trip to the coast! Train leaves London at 08.00 and breakfast is served before you arrive at Poole Harbour. There you have the rest of the day to watch the ferries or take a fishing trip. Supper is served on the return journey arriving back in London at 20.30 hours.

9

[Turn over

Part 3

Questions 11–20

- Look at the statements below about Health Advice for Travellers.
- Read the text on the opposite page to decide if each statement is correct or incorrect.
- If it is correct, mark **A on your answer sheet.**
- If it is not correct, mark **B on your answer sheet.**

Example answer:

11   The best time to get medical help is a month before you leave.

12   A doctor can tell you which drugs can be taken through customs.

13   You should go to your dentist before departure if necessary.

14   You should never use tap water for cleaning your teeth.

15   Raw vegetables are safer than cooked ones.

16   Sunbathing is safe if you use sun cream.

17   You should avoid wearing clothes which are too tight.

18   An insect bite, unlike an animal bite, is not serious.

19   If you see a doctor abroad, you should see another one when you return.

20   It is important to remember which countries you visit.

HEALTH ADVICE FOR TRAVELLERS TO TROPICAL COUNTRIES

Be well prepared so you can enjoy your stay!

You can get information about the country you are visiting from your travel agent or each country's Embassy. If you think you will need special medical advice then you should see your doctor at least two months before your departure. If you want to take any medicines abroad with you, then find out from your local chemist if you are allowed to take them into the country you're visiting.

If you've got any doubts about your teeth, see your dentist as it may be difficult or expensive to get help abroad.

Take a small first aid kit with you; it will not take up much space and could be very useful

Also check the water you use for cleaning your teeth and washing your mouth.

Unless you know it is safe always try and use bottled water.

Be careful with the following foods: raw vegetables, salads, unpeeled fruit, raw shellfish, cream, ice-cream, undercooked meat or fish. It is also not a good idea to eat food which has been cooked, left to go cold and then heated up again. Freshly cooked foods are safer.

More than anything, holiday makers go abroad to find the sun. However, the sun may be much more powerful abroad than what you are used to in your own country. Take care not to lie in the sun for too long, especially in the early days.

The sun can burn your skin even if you use sun creams and cause your body to overheat. Even when you can avoid direct sun, temperatures may be very

high. Try not to do anything too energetic in the hottest hours. Wear light, loose clothing and have plenty to drink. Bathing in the sea will cool you, but remember that accidents happen very easily.

If you are walking in wooded areas and you get bitten or scratched then go to the nearest hospital immediately. A bite from an animal or an insect can lead to illness even if it does not seem dangerous at the time. Even if you receive medical help and you are feeling fit, you should visit your own doctor as soon as you get back to your country.

If you become ill when you come back, tell your doctor which countries you have stayed in or travelled through. He or she will then quickly be able to check whether you will need specialist medical help.

[Turn over

Part 4

Questions 21–25

● Read the text and questions below.

● For each question, mark the letter next to the correct answer – **A**, **B**, **C** or **D** – **on your answer sheet**.

Example answer: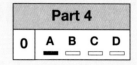

In the past few years ballooning has become a popular sport in the UK. Although it is still quite expensive compared with other sports, many people now think of a balloon flight as the perfect answer for a birthday present or a particular occasion. Some businesses also entertain their staff or visitors with a balloon ride and may even buy their own balloon to advertise their business products.

One of the best known balloon companies in the UK is based in Bristol in the west of England. Flights are available throughout the year and last for at least one hour. They usually take off soon after sunrise or a couple of hours before sunset, but they do not fly if it is raining or very windy. No special clothing is necessary other than outdoor clothing and either walking shoes or boots.

It seems that once people have experienced a balloon flight they can become so keen on the sport that they want to have their own balloon. No two flights are ever the same and people find the sport different and exciting. The company in Bristol trains people to fly their own balloons but warns that it can be a very expensive hobby.

21 What is the writer trying to do in the text?

   A   to tell a story about ballooning

   B   to advertise a new sport

   C   to give information on ballooning

   D   to recommend a new sport

22 Why would somebody read the text?

   A   to learn about a dangerous sport

   B   to find out about joining a club

   C   to know more about ballooning

   D   to find out about ballooning costs

23   Why could an interest in ballooning almost be a disadvantage?

   A   People can become addicts.

   B   People lose a lot of money.

   C   It leads to business difficulties.

   D   It is bad for one's health.

24   What do we learn from the text about ballooning?

   A   It's best for business advertising.

   B   It has become dearer recently.

   C   It can only be done during the summer.

   D   It is considered to be rather special.

25   Which of these letters did the writer send to a friend?

A

... it was marvellous. We took off early in the morning before the sun was up and flew for miles. It rained quite a lot but it didn't seem to matter ...

B

... it was dark when we took off but fortunately there was a strong wind. It was quite cold but we had special clothing to keep us warm ...

C

... so we wore only ordinary clothes and flat shoes. The views were wonderful, and it was so early that the world below looked completely empty apart from us ...

D

... each day we flew the same route, leaving just before daylight. The flights lasted about an hour although I wished we could have stayed up longer ...

[Turn over

Part 5

Questions 26–35

● Read the text below and choose the correct word for each space.

● For each question, mark the letter next to the correct word – **A**, **B**, **C** or **D** – **on your answer sheet**.

Example answer:

	Part 5			
0	A	B	C	D

ART FACTORIES

Several years ago an old factory on the edge of Paris was turned (**0**)............ an exhibition centre. This helped many artists (**26**)............ had found it too expensive to work in the centre of Paris, and so for the (**27**)............ few years painters, musicians, actors and other people (**28**)........... had space to work and perform. The people behind the idea now (**29**)............ to change the use of other old buildings (**30**)............ the same reasons. Sometimes the use of the buildings can only (**31**)............ for a short period of time, a year for example, (**32**)............ the opportunity is always worth it for the young artists. On one occasion a businessman lent an old building (**33**)............ the organisers for two years, and in that time the artists were (**34**)............ to put on concerts, art exhibitions and fashion shows to (**35**)............ the local people.

0	**A**	into	**B**	onto	**C**	up	**D**	out
26	**A**	which	**B**	some	**C**	who	**D**	those
27	**A**	other	**B**	past	**C**	late	**D**	remaining
28	**A**	have	**B**	must	**C**	would	**D**	had
29	**A**	think	**B**	like	**C**	go	**D**	want
30	**A**	with	**B**	by	**C**	beyond	**D**	for
31	**A**	take	**B**	be	**C**	seem	**D**	have
32	**A**	but	**B**	so	**C**	because	**D**	since
33	**A**	for	**B**	in	**C**	to	**D**	from
34	**A**	suitable	**B**	able	**C**	better	**D**	successful
35	**A**	attract	**B**	bring	**C**	provide	**D**	enjoy

14

Writing

Part 1

Questions 1–5

- Here are some sentences about a family restaurant.
- For each question, finish the second sentence so that it means the same as the first.
- The second sentence is started for you. **Write only the missing words on your answer sheet**.
- You may use this page for any rough work.

Example: Children's meals are free if they are under five.

Children under five *do not have to pay for their meals.*

1   There is plenty to choose from the menu.

   There is plenty of ....

2   We have special seats for very young children.

   There ....

3   There is a new menu daily.

   Every ....

4   Hot and cold dishes are included on the menu.

   The menu ....

5   Family tables can be reserved.

   You ....

[Turn over

Part 2

Questions 6–15

- You want to join an international friendship club.
- The club has sent you their application form.
- Look at the form and answer each question.
- **Write your answers on your answer sheet.**
- You may use this page for any rough work.

INTERNATIONAL FRIENDSHIP CLUB

22 Palmer Buildings Highampton HG1 6DE

Application Form for Membership

Surname: **(6)** ....

First name: **(7)** ....

Address: **(8)** ....

Nationality: **(9)** ....

Date of birth (day/month/year): **(10)** ....

Which languages can you speak?

(11) ....

What are your hobbies?

(12) ....

Why do you want to join the Club?

(13) ....

How long have you been learning English?

(14) ....

Signature: **(15)** ....

Part 3

Question 16

● An English-speaking friend is coming to stay with you for the weekend.

● Write a letter telling your friend about three ideas you have for her/his visit.

● **Finish the letter on your answer sheet, using about 100 words.**

● You may use this page for any rough work.

Dear

I am looking forward to seeing you soon. ....

....

....

....

....

....

....

....

....

....

PAPER 2
Listening Test

(30 minutes + 12 minutes transfer time)

Part 1

Questions 1–7

● There are seven questions in this Part.
● For each question there are four pictures and a short recording.
● You will hear each recording twice.
● For each question, look at the pictures and listen to the recording.
● Choose the correct picture and put a tick (✓) in the box below it.

Example: What time is the match?

A ✓   B ☐   C ☐   D ☐

1   Where is Maria?

A ☐   B ☐   C ☐   D ☐

2   What are they going to eat?

A ☐   B ☐   C ☐   D ☐

3   Where are the two friends going to meet?

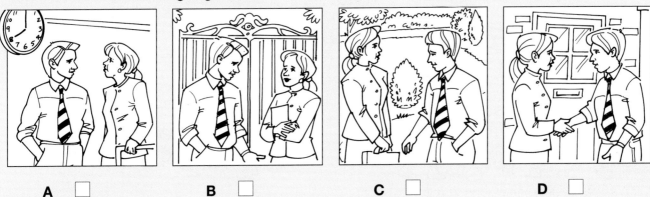

A ☐   B ☐   C ☐   D ☐

4   Which picture is their mother?

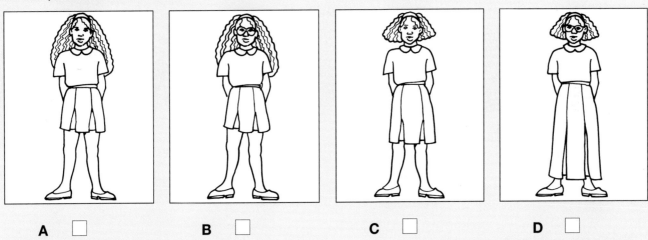

A ☐   B ☐   C ☐   D ☐

5   What has happened to the boy's bike?

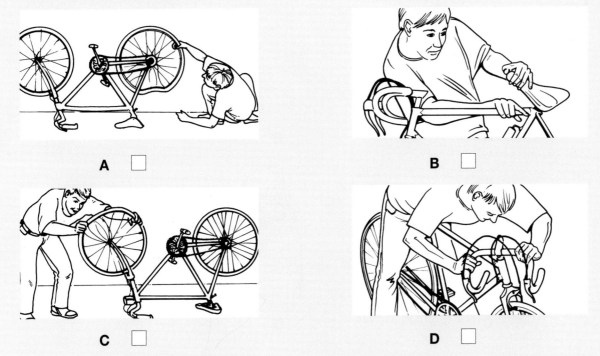

A ☐   B ☐

C ☐   D ☐

[Turn over

6   Where did the man spend his holiday?

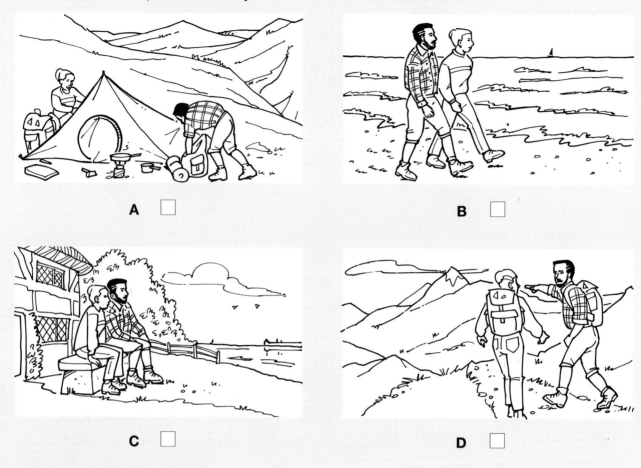

A ☐

B ☐

C ☐

D ☐

7   What's the problem?

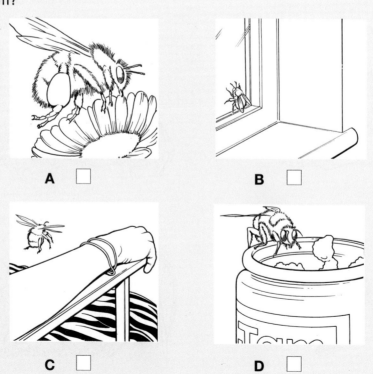

A ☐

B ☐

C ☐

D ☐

Part 2

Questions 8–13

● Look at the questions for this Part.
● You will hear a woman giving details about the week's activities at a summer camp.
● Put a tick (✓) in the correct box for each question.

8   The rock climbing class meets

A ☐ by the pool.

B ☐ in the car park.

C ☐ by the tennis courts.

D ☐ in the gym.

9   Lunch starts at

A ☐ 12.00.

B ☐ 12.30.

C ☐ 13.00.

D ☐ 13.30.

10   The horse riding group

A ☐ leaves from the bus stop.

B ☐ arrives back at the main gate.

C ☐ has to walk back from the lesson.

D ☐ returns by bus for lunch.

11   Disco dance classes are held in the

A ☐ open air.

B ☐ practice rooms.

C ☐ music studio.

D ☐ drama hall.

12   If you want to change your course you must

A ☐ sign another form.

B ☐ inform your teacher.

C ☐ tell your group leader.

D ☐ wait until the evening.

13   In good weather

A ☐ everyone is given a picnic lunch.

B ☐ lunch is cooked out of doors.

C ☐ everyone can take their trays outside.

D ☐ group leaders bring a picnic.

[Turn over

Part 3

Questions 14–19

- Look at the notes about some things which are being advertised for sale on a radio programme.
- Some information is missing.
- You will hear different people talking about what they want to sell.
- For each question, fill in the missing information in the numbered space.

RADIO 749 SHOP WINDOW

First caller – Isabel

Wants to sell a (14) . . . .

Paid £500, wants £200.

Size: (15) . . . .

Ring 491268

Second caller – Tony

Selling a (16) . . . .

Price: -around £65.

Address: 21 (17) . . . .

Call round after 6pm

Third caller – Ted

Wants to sell his (18) . . . .

Price: £340

Colours: (19) . . . .

Ring 73155 any time

Part 4

Questions 20–25

● Look at the six statements for this Part.
● You will hear a conversation between a garage owner and a woman who recently bought a car from him.
● Decide if you think each statement is correct or incorrect.
● If you think it is correct, put a tick (✓) in the box under **A** for **YES**. If you think it is not correct, put a tick (✓) in the box under **B** for **NO**.

		A YES	B NO
20	The woman is pleased with her new car.	☐	☐
21	The man is surprised by what the woman says.	☐	☐
22	The woman keeps her car in the garage at night.	☐	☐
23	The woman insists that her car needs checking.	☐	☐
24	The garage wants the car for a whole day.	☐	☐
25	The man agrees the woman can borrow a car.	☐	☐

Speaking Test

Part 1	**General conversation (2–3 minutes)**
Tasks	Identifying oneself, giving information about people, asking direct questions.
Sub tasks	Spelling, numbers, responding to questions and information.
	Ask each other questions to find out information about personal details, family, home town, schools, jobs, etc.

Part 2	**Simulated situation (2–3 minutes)**
Tasks	Making plans, agreeing and disagreeing, asking for and giving opinions.
	You have been asked to organize a day trip for your English class together.
	Look at picture 1 on page 25.
	Talk about what you would like to do and what preparations you will have to make.

Part 3	**Responding to a visual stimulus** **(5 minutes for Parts 3 and 4 together)**
Tasks	Describing people and places, saying where people are and what they are doing.
	Candidate A should look at picture 1 on page 111, show it to Candidate B and talk about it.
	Candidate B should look at picture 1 on page 112, show it to Candidate A and talk about it.

Part 4	**General conversation (based on the photographs)**
Tasks	Talking about one's likes and dislikes, expressing opinions.
	Talk to each other about spending time with friends or members of your family. Talk about the kinds of things you like or dislike doing with your friends, and the things which you like or dislike doing with your family.

PAPER 1
Reading and Writing Test

(1 hour 30 minutes)

Reading

Part 1

Questions 1–5

● Look at the sign in each question.
● Someone asks you what it means.
● Mark the letter next to the correct explanation – **A**, **B**, **C** or **D** – **on your answer sheet**.

Example:

0

A Come in whenever you like.

B Please ring for an appointment.

C We will call you when we are free.

D Visitors please wait outside.

Example answer:

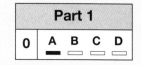

Part 1			
0 A	B	C	D

1

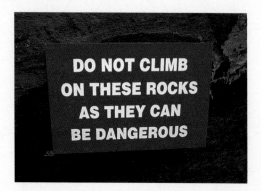

A Stay away because the rocks are unsafe.

B Be careful of these sharp rocks.

C Don't climb these rocks without a guide.

D Mind you don't fall off these rocks.

2

A   You are advised to wait here for an assistant.

B   You should ask if you want someone to help you.

C   Please help yourself if our assistants are busy.

D   Our assistants are pleased to receive any advice.

3

A   You must play your radio very quietly in the gardens.

B   You must not bring radios into the gardens.

C   Do not leave your radio in these gardens.

D   Radios cannot be played in these gardens.

4

A   Please help children to cross here safely.

B   This area is dangerous unless you can swim.

C   Stop children going too near the water.

D   This water is not safe for drinking.

5

A   This door must be left open during the day.

B   When you leave, this door should remain open.

C   You must check this door is shut when you depart.

D   Please leave the key behind when you go.

[Turn over

Part 2

Questions 6–10

- The people below are trying to choose which TV programme to watch.
- On the opposite page there are descriptions of eight TV programmes.
- Decide which programme (**letters A–H**) would be the most suitable for each person (**numbers 6–10**).
- For each of those numbers mark the correct letter **on your answer sheet**.

Example answer:

Part 2								
0	A	B	C	D	E	F	G	H
	▬	☐	☐	☐	☐	☐	☐	☐

6

Although Rob leads a quiet life in a small village, that doesn't stop him from wanting to find out about the latest scientific developments.

7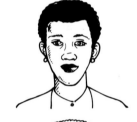

Bella enjoys eating out but can't afford to spend very much at the moment as she is saving for a holiday. She has never learnt how to cook, so now might be quite a good time to find out!

8

Dan is interested in taking wildlife photographs and enjoys any kind of programme which gives him a chance to see a professional photographer at work.

9

Gina is a music teacher. Although she prefers classical music she likes to follow the kind of music that interests the teenagers she teaches.

10

Ron's wife is in hospital. He wants to find a programme suitable for his three-year-old son while he gets on with the housework and prepares a meal.

TODAY'S TELEVISION PROGRAMME
PREVIEW

A

TV 3

5.30 pm   An hour-long children's programme presented by Terri Greene. Today's programme includes a documentary on Eastern Europe plus a look at one of the world's great orchestras in rehearsal. Also a new competition for children at secondary school.

B

TV 1

7.20 pm   Find out more about Australia's animal life. This film was made last year by one of Australia's best-known cameramen, Dougie Bond. He spent over 200 hours filming the birds, animals and fish that inhabit this beautiful continent and for the first time brings some of these unusual animals to our TV screens.

C

TV 3

9.00 pm   The popular science programme is back with the latest in technology and medicine. This week, cars that run on sunlight and the story of one baby's fight to live.

D

TV 2

6.10 pm   Do you stop to think what goes into the food most of us eat every day of the week? Tonight's programme takes a serious scientific look at the bread industry. Whether you bake your own bread or just enjoy buying it, this programme will give you an interesting insight into something most of us eat every day of the week.

E

TV 1

5.15 pm   Busy parents? Bored children? Do you want something educational to entertain your children while you do something else? This popular magazine programme is for the under-fives. More music, fun, songs and games with Carla and Larry.

F

TV 3

6.45 pm   If you've always wanted to cook, now's your chance to learn. In the studio are two chefs who will take you through some simple recipes step by step. This is a repeat of the popular series shown last year, and a recipe book to accompany the series is available from most good bookshops.

G

TV 2

8.00 pm   Village life differs all over the world. Today's programme comes from Ghana in West Africa. Beautifully filmed, it follows one day in the life of the Acheampong family. There is also a chance to see some Ghanaian wildlife – snakes such as the green mamba and the spitting cobra which may just lie across your path on the way to market!

H

TV 3

7.40 pm   The latest new music. Pete Hogg looks at the best of the current rap, ragga and new jack swing plus new video releases. This is the programme that tells you all about what's happening on the music scene and brings you interviews with tomorrow's young artists.

[Turn over

Part 3

Questions 11–20

● Look at the statements below about the Hotel Alpha.

● Read the text on the opposite page to decide if each statement is correct or incorrect.

● If it is correct, mark **A on your answer sheet.**

● If it is not correct, mark **B on your answer sheet.**

Example answer:

11   I will probably be able to park my car under cover.

12   I can check in late in the evening.

13   All single rooms have their own bathroom.

14   I can have something to eat if I arrive after 23.00 hours.

15   I need to bring my own hair-dryer.

16   I can have a full breakfast in my room.

17   I can have breakfast before 07.00 hours.

18   I must reserve a table if I want dinner.

19   I have to pay to use the swimming pool.

20   I can take my dog to my room.

Hotel Alpha

- Hotel Alpha is situated close to the motorway and within 2 kilometres of Newton city centre. The hotel has 220 car parking spaces as well as 15 lock-up garages. Overnight charges are available on request.

- There is a 24-hour reception service which means you can check in whenever you want. Fax and photocopying services are available on request at Reception.

- We offer both single and double rooms. All our rooms are comfortably furnished; most rooms have either a shower or a bath and all double rooms have their own bathrooms.

- All rooms have a phone and mini-bar and guests are welcome to watch TV in the lounge. Room service is available after 21.00 until midnight; drinks and sandwiches may be ordered by dialling 91. If you wish to order a newspaper please inform Reception the night before.

- Each room has a radio/alarm clock but you can order a wake-up call from Reception for a small extra charge.

- There is a hair-dryer in each room but if you wish to use an iron please contact the housekeeper on each floor who will be pleased to help you. Small toilet items such as toothpaste may be bought from the housekeeper.

- Breakfast is served from 06.30 to 10.00. Help yourself to as much as you like from our breakfast buffet. A light continental breakfast can be served in your room but this must be ordered the night before.

- The Alpha restaurant is open for lunch from midday until 14.00 hours. Choose from a range of hot and cold dishes as well as the daily Chef's Special. Dinner is served from 19.00 - 21.00 and as we are always busy it is a good idea to book a table if you want to be sure of a place. The restaurant is not open to non- residents although guests are welcome to entertain personal visitors.

- Hotel Alpha has the following sports facilities: indoor swimming pool, multi-gym, table tennis and snooker rooms. Guests who wish to use these facilities, which are free of charge, are asked to make arrangements through Reception. There is an early morning swimming session between 07.00 and 9.00 after which the pool is closed until midday.

- Guests are not allowed to bring pets into the hotel but for a small fee we can arrange for animals to be looked after nearby. Please let us know in advance if you wish to bring an animal with you.

[Turn over

Activate Learning

Part 4

Questions 21–25

● Read the text and questions below.

● For each question, mark the letter next to the correct answer – **A, B, C** or **D** – **on your answer sheet**.

Example answer:
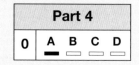

Part 4				
0	A	B	C	D
	▬	▭	▭	▭

… and we were sorry to hear about the accident. Anyway, you mustn't feel too anxious about work. A lot of people are away on holiday this month, so there's not as much business as usual.

When you are feeling a little better we'd like to come and see you; we'll bring you some of your favourite chocolates – promise!

Now for office news. Have you heard that the boss is getting married again next month? She tried to keep it quiet but one of the secretaries heard her talking about wedding arrangements over the phone, so now of course everyone knows! We're collecting money to buy her a present. It's really difficult to know what to get her as she has most things. Someone has suggested theatre or concert tickets, which is a good idea. We can find out from her personal assistant what her plans are and when she has a free evening. The only problem is that although we know what she likes, we don't know whether her future husband shares her tastes.

All being well, we'll see you some time next week. Until then we all send our good wishes and hope you recover quickly.

21 What is the writer trying to do in the text?

    A   to give some cheerful news

    B   to offer professional advice

    C   to describe her office work

    D   to suggest ways to recover

22 Why would somebody read the text?

    A   to find out about a wedding present

    B   to arrange to see friends

    C   to learn about a person's accident

    D   to help them stop worrying

23   What does the writer suggest about one of the secretaries?

   A   She's hard-working.

   B   She talks too much.

   C   She likes secrets.

   D   She enjoys weddings.

24   Why is it difficult to buy the boss a present?

   A   She already has a lot of things.

   B   No one knows her fiancé.

   C   They haven't much money.

   D   She's been married once before.

25   Which of the cards below do you think the writer sent?

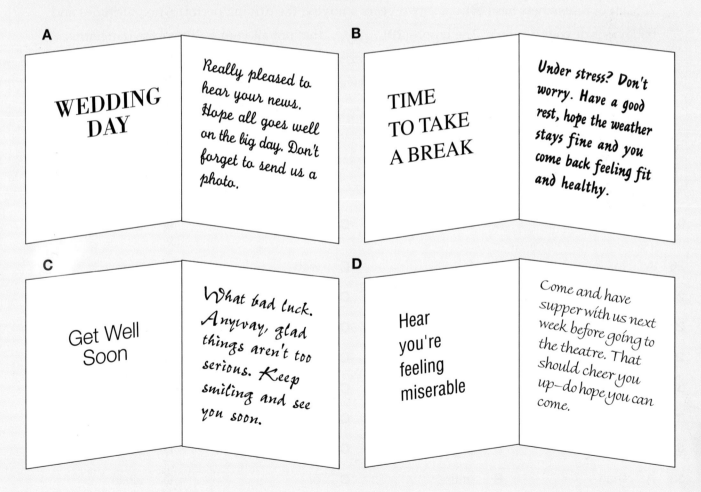

A

WEDDING DAY

Really pleased to hear your news. Hope all goes well on the big day. Don't forget to send us a photo.

B

TIME TO TAKE A BREAK

Under stress? Don't worry. Have a good rest, hope the weather stays fine and you come back feeling fit and healthy.

C

Get Well Soon

What bad luck. Anyway, glad things aren't too serious. Keep smiling and see you soon.

D

Hear you're feeling miserable

Come and have supper with us next week before going to the theatre. That should cheer you up – do hope you can come.

[Turn over

Part 5

Questions 26–35

● Read the text below and choose the correct word for each space.

● For each question, mark the letter next to the correct word – **A**, **B**, **C** or **D** – **on your answer sheet.**

Example answer:

Part 5				
0	A	B	C	D

YOUTH AT THE WHEEL

One in six drivers in Britain is aged between 17 and 25. But more drivers in (**0**)............ age group are responsible (**26**)............ a greater number of accidents than older drivers; in (**27**)............ one accident in four is the fault of a young, inexperienced driver.

A team of researchers has (**28**)........... two years studying the driving performance, attitudes and behaviour of young people. The report (**29**)............ that not all young drivers are dangerous, (**30**)............ a large number of males, particularly those aged 17 to 20, do not drive as carefully (**31**)............ other age groups. These young drivers are more likely to have (**32**)............ accident in their first year of driving (**33**)............ when their experience increases. The report also notes that men are more likely to (**34**)............ driving rules than women, and that a girlfriend or wife in the car has a calming (**35**)............ on the driving pattern of young men.

0	**A**	this	**B**	some	**C**	one	**D**	that
26	**A**	to	**B**	for	**C**	with	**D**	from
27	**A**	order	**B**	place	**C**	time	**D**	fact
28	**A**	done	**B**	put	**C**	given	**D**	spent
29	**A**	says	**B**	tells	**C**	speaks	**D**	talks
30	**A**	and	**B**	but	**C**	since	**D**	because
31	**A**	so	**B**	like	**C**	as	**D**	that
32	**A**	the	**B**	this	**C**	an	**D**	some
33	**A**	than	**B**	until	**C**	or	**D**	while
34	**A**	crash	**B**	break	**C**	tear	**D**	escape
35	**A**	way	**B**	effort	**C**	method	**D**	influence

Writing

Part 1

Questions 1–5

- Here are some sentences about a new sports centre.
- For each question, finish the second sentence so that it means the same as the first.
- The second sentence is started for you. **Write only the missing words on your answer sheet.**
- You may use this page for any rough work.

Example: A new sports centre was opened by the president last week.

The president *opened a new sports centre last week.*

1 There are two separate swimming pools.

   It ....

2 The main pool is just for adults.

   Only adults ....

3 Entry is free if you are under 18.

   You ....

4 Sports equipment can be hired.

   You ....

5 Swimming is very good for your health.

   Swimming keeps ....

[Turn over

Part 2

Questions 6–15

● You are going to take part in a family exchange programme.
● You have received this application form.
● Look at the form and answer each question.
● **Write your answers on your answer sheet**.
● You may use this page for any rough work.

FAMILY EXCHANGE QUESTIONNAIRE

Home Stays
1 Richmond Avenue
Bentwood
BW4 3LD

Full name: (**6**) ....

Home address: (**7**)...

Nationality: (**8**) ....

Date of birth (day/month/year): (**9**) ....

Sex: (**10**)...

How long have you been learning English?

(**11**) ....

What are your hobbies/interests?

(**12**) ....

Why do you want to stay with a foreign family?

(**13**) ....

Have you any special requests?

(**14**) ....

Signature: (**15**) ....

Part 3

Question 16

● Last month you and your family moved to a new house in another town.
● You are writing a letter to an English-speaking friend to tell her/him about your new house, neighbours, and the area.
● **Finish the letter on your answer sheet, using about 100 words.**
● You may use this page for any rough work.

Dear

We finally moved house last month and now life has really changed. ....

....

....

....

....

....

....

....

....

....

PAPER 2
Listening Test

(30 minutes + 12 minutes transfer time)

Part 1

Questions 1–7

● There are seven questions in this Part.
● For each question there are four pictures and a short recording.
● You will hear each recording twice.
● For each question, look at the pictures and listen to the recording.
● Choose the correct picture and put a tick (✓) in the box below it.

Example: What time is the match?

A ✓   B ☐   C ☐   D ☐

1   What happened at the airport?

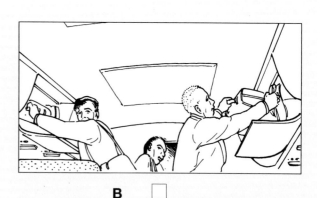

A ☐   B ☐

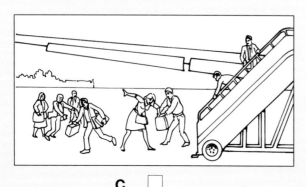

C ☐   D ☐

2 What does the flag look like?

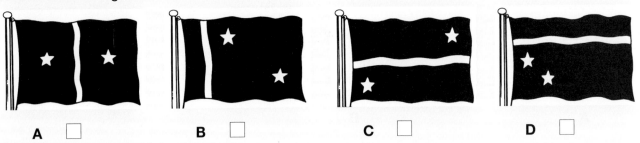

A ☐   **B** ☐   **C** ☐   **D** ☐

3 What are they watching?

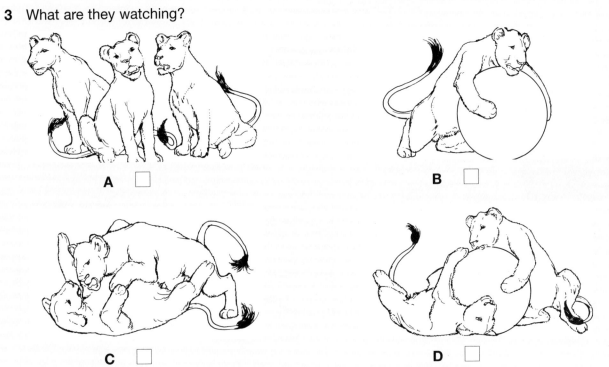

A ☐   **B** ☐

C ☐   **D** ☐

4 What did she buy?

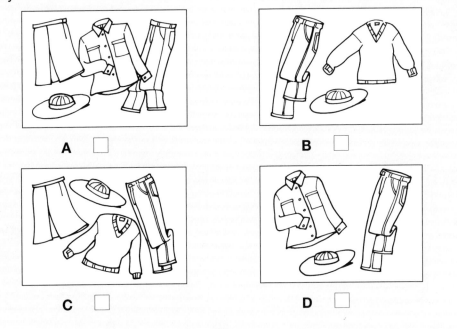

A ☐   **B** ☐

C ☐   **D** ☐

39   **[Turn over**

5 Where's the flour?

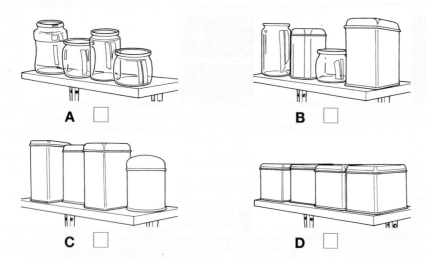

A ☐   B ☐

C ☐   D ☐

6 What's the weather going to be like?

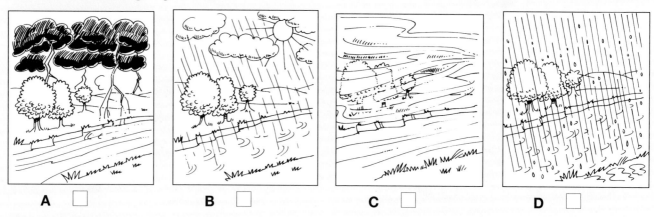

A ☐   B ☐   C ☐   D ☐

7 What happened?

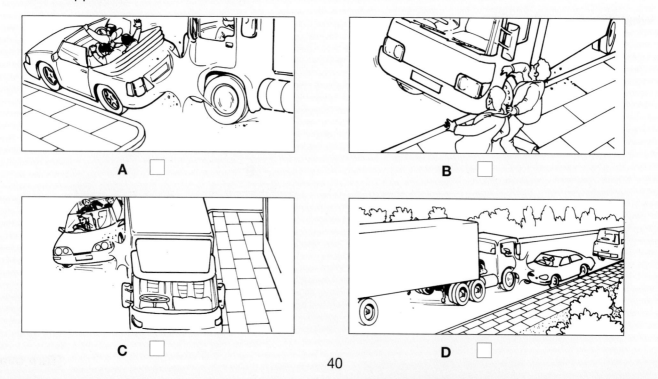

A ☐   B ☐

C ☐   D ☐

Part 2

Questions 8–13

● Look at the questions for this Part.
● You will hear a radio programme which recommends somewhere to stay for a short holiday.
● Put a tick (✓) in the correct box for each question.

8   Ternmouth is

A ☐ a country town.

B ☐ a small city.

C ☐ an industrial capital.

D ☐ a large port.

9   Why do people usually go to Ternmouth?

A ☐ It has plenty of cheap shops.

B ☐ It's on their holiday route.

C ☐ It's a popular holiday place.

D ☐ It's got excellent hotels.

10   Some of Ternmouth's fish restaurants

A ☐ are good value for money.

B ☐ look out onto the cliffs.

C ☐ serve hot food all day.

D ☐ are built in the old town.

11   The old town has hotels

A ☐ without car parking spaces.

B ☐ just offering bed and breakfast.

C ☐ which are quiet but expensive.

D ☐ with large popular restaurants.

12   If you want to stay at a cliff-top hotel you

A ☐ take the hotel mini-bus.

B ☐ should go by car.

C ☐ can park very easily.

D ☐ get the bus from the centre.

13   The tourist office phone number is

A ☐ 202618.

B ☐ 220186.

C ☐ 202816.

D ☐ 220816.

[Turn over

Part 3

Questions 14–19

● Look at the notes about stolen property.
● Some information is missing.
● You will hear a college director talking to some students about what has been stolen.
● For each question, fill in the missing information in the numbered space.

WILTON COLLEGE BREAK-IN

(14).. broken into.

College director has been in contact with

(15)..

Stolen objects include:

(16).. given to Wilton years ago,

(17).. by Arnolfini,

(18).. - very old, TV and video recorder,

(19).. stolen from filing cabinet.

Part 4

Questions 20–25

● Look at the six statements for this Part.
● You will hear a conversation between a woman called Sally and a man called Karl who are making plans for a party.
● Decide if you think each statement is correct or incorrect.
● If you think it is correct, put a tick (✓) in the box under **A** for **YES**. If you think it is not correct, put a tick (✓) in the box under **B** for **NO**.

		A YES	B NO
20	Sally thinks their neighbours are dull.	☐	☐
21	The guests will help by bringing food.	☐	☐
22	Karl has already planned what to eat.	☐	☐
23	Sally enjoys chicken with rice and fruit.	☐	☐
24	Sally thinks watching a video would spoil the party.	☐	☐
25	Karl promises to find a suitable video.	☐	☐

Speaking Test

Part 1	**General conversation (2–3 minutes)**
Tasks	Identifying oneself, giving information about people, asking direct questions.
Sub tasks	Spelling, numbers, responding to questions and information.
	Ask each other questions to find out information about personal details, family, home town, schools, jobs, etc.
Part 2	**Simulated situation (2–3 minutes)**
Tasks	Stating preferences, agreeing and disagreeing, making choices.
	One of your teachers is leaving to work in another school. You have to decide what to buy her/him as a leaving present.
	Look at picture 1 on page 45.
	Discuss the different ideas and then decide what would make the best present.
Part 3	**Responding to a visual stimulus** **(5 minutes for Parts 3 and 4 together)**
Tasks	Describing people and places, saying where people are and what they are doing.
	Candidate A should look at picture 1 on page 65, show it to Candidate B and talk about it.
	Candidate B should look at picture 2 on page 111, show it to Candidate A and talk about it.
Part 4	**General conversation (based on the photographs)**
Tasks	Talking about likes and dislikes, expressing opinions.
	Talk to each other about the kind of holiday you enjoy. Talk about the ways you like or dislike travelling and the kinds of places you like to stay at when you go on holiday.

Picture 1

Picture 2

45

PAPER 1
Reading and Writing Test

(1 hour 30 minutes)

Reading

Part 1

Questions 1–5

● Look at the sign in each question.
● Someone asks you what it means.
● Mark the letter next to the correct explanation – **A**, **B**, **C** or **D** – **on your answer sheet.**

Example:

0

A Come in whenever you like.

B Please ring for an appointment.

C We will call you when we are free.

D Visitors please wait outside.

Example answer:

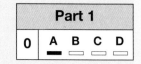

Part 1				
0	A	B	C	D

1

A You can write your cheque at this pay desk.

B You must use a credit card if you pay here.

C You may cash your cheque at this pay desk.

D You do not need to write your own cheque details.

2

A Performances start an hour later this week.

B The theatre closes when the performance begins.

C Performances are every half an hour.

D Performances start half an hour after the theatre opens.

3

A No driver can cross without first phoning.

B Certain vehicles are not allowed to cross here.

C Some drivers will need to phone before they cross.

D You should cross here if you need the phone.

4

A These chairs are reserved for visitors.

B You need a ticket to sit here.

C These chairs must not be touched.

D These chairs have already been sold.

5

A Waste paper should be put in the basket.

B This basket is full of waste paper.

C Do not use the paper in this basket.

D This basket must not be used for paper.

[Turn over

Part 2

Questions 6–10

● The people below all want to buy a magazine.

● On the opposite page there are descriptions of eight magazines.

● Decide which magazine (**letters A–H**) would be the most suitable for each person (**numbers 6–10**).

● For each of those numbers mark the correct letter **on your answer sheet**.

Example answer:

Part 2								
0	A	B	C	D	E	F	G	H
	▬	▭	▭	▭	▭	▭	▭	▭

6

Emi is at university studying Italian and Politics. She doesn't have much time to read anything very detailed but she is looking for something with plenty of news and information.

7

Carrie is sixteen years old and loves spending time listening to pop music and lying on her bed reading. She is always interested in finding out more about some of the stars in the worlds of pop and fashion.

8

Bill travelled a lot when he was younger. Now that he has stopped work he enjoys reading about foreign people, places and customs even if he has already visited that part of the world.

9

Leroy used to be a detective. He still takes an active interest in the work of the police, but these days he enjoys reading fiction after years spent chasing real criminals.

10

Up till now Brigitte has never travelled far but this year she has decided to go abroad for the first time. The travel agent suggests that she reads about various countries first before choosing her holiday.

A

DETECTIVES ABROAD

Read about the lives of real detectives. This monthly magazine brings you up-to-date true stories about real life detectives as they chase criminals across continents. Find out how some of the most dangerous criminals in the world are caught by some of the world's finest detectives. Follow their routes on the free map which comes with every issue.

B

WORLD TRAVEL magazine

The weekly magazine that brings the world to your home. Have you ever wondered what the Chinese eat for breakfast? Did you know that the Sahara desert is getting bigger every year? This fascinating magazine, full of colour photographs, is your window on the world.

C

Only 16
....

Every week well-known writers bring you the latest in teenage love stories. Each magazine carries three full-length stories as well as cartoons and colour pictures of your favourite film stars.

D

EUROPEAN WEEKLY

A magazine that gives you in-depth articles on a different subject each week. Various top journalists – specialists in the subject area – bring you the best in political journalism for the serious reader. Order it from your newsagent now!

E

EUROPA NEWS

The weekly magazine that keeps you in touch with what's happening. Filled with facts and figures about almost everything you can think of, plus articles by our regular writers on the week's most interesting news stories. Special back page sums up the news for the busy reader.

F

Teenage Lifeline

If you want to be part of the scene then Teenage Lifeline is a must. Do you want to know who's wearing what? Where to shop for the cheapest and the best in clothes, CDs, videos and posters? You name it and we write about it. Buy it today!

G

Foreign Parts

The weekly magazine which tells you all you need to know if you're thinking of travelling. Helpful advice on what to pack and what to buy once you're there. Lots of colour photos to help you choose the best hotel, the cheapest flights and a special guide to different climates each week.

H

CRIME AND CRIMINALS

These exciting short stories are written by well-known crime writers. Every magazine brings you the best in criminal thrillers, stories that are so good that you won't be able to put the magazine down! And every month we leave one crime unanswered so that you, the reader, can play detective.

[Turn over

Part 3

Questions 11–20

- Look at the statements below about the Griffith Observatory.
- Read the text on the opposite page to decide if each statement is correct or incorrect.
- If it is correct, mark **A on your answer sheet**.
- If it is not correct, mark **B on your answer sheet**.

Example answer:

11   The Observatory was bought by Los Angeles City.

12   The Observatory opened in the thirties.

13   Shows at the Planetarium last two hours.

14   Tours at the Hall of Science have to be booked.

15   Children under five will have to pay for some shows.

16   Both the Planetarium and the Hall of Science close at 10 p.m.

17   School groups need to book their visits.

18   You can buy videos in the Space Stop.

19   The *Griffith Observer* is printed once a month.

20   The *Griffith Observer* has news about the US space program.

GRIFFITH OBSERVATORY

The Griffith Observatory and the park in which it is located were made possible by a generous present from Colonel Griffith to the City of Los Angeles. The Observatory has been visited by over 50 million people since opening its doors in 1935. The Observatory is operated by the Department of Recreation and Parks.

The Observatory is located at the north end of Vermont Avenue on the south slope of Mount Hollywood in Griffith Park.

Planetarium

The Planetarium is a large theatre where, with the help of a Zeiss projector, you are transported to different parts of the universe. All the shows are very dramatic and full of interest and usually last one hour. Subjects change several times a year. Call for further information.

Planetarium Hours

Summer and holidays

Mon. – Fri.	1.30, 3.00, 7.30
Sat. & Sun.	1.30, 3.00, 4.30, 7.30

Winter

Tue. – Fri.	3.00, 7.30
Sat. & Sun.	1.30, 3.00, 4.30, 7.30
Mon.	Closed

Planetarium Admission

Children (5–12)	$2.00
General (13–64)	$4.00
Seniors (65 and older)	$3.50

Children under 5 are allowed only to the 1.30 planetarium show and to special children's shows. Children under 5 will be charged an entry fee for certain shows. There is no charge to the Hall of Science.

School Programs

Special morning planetarium shows are offered to school groups during the year. Entry fee is $1.00 per person.

Phone only between 7.45 and 9.45am Tuesday through Friday for additional information. Reservations are required.

Hall of Science

Arrive early to allow time to tour the Hall of Science. The exhibits include a Solar Telescope, Meteorites and many more. Tours are given at regular intervals.

Summer	Every day	12.30pm – 10.00pm
Winter	Tue. – Fri.	2.00pm – 10.00pm
	Sat. & Sun.	12.30pm – 10.00pm
	Mon.	Closed

Laserium

Laserium sound and light concerts are given every evening after the planetarium show. Attending both the planetarium show and Laserium gives you easy parking and reserved seats.

Book Shop and Space Stop

Be sure to visit Griffith Observatory Book Shop and Space Stop gift areas. Both have a choice of books and posters and unusual presents.

Special Activities

The Observatory offers a variety of short courses and popular lectures.

Griffith Observer

Enjoy the Observatory's own monthly magazine. Read articles by famous writers who will thrill you with stories out of this world. Each issue comes with detailed maps and information to help you look at the night sky.

Friends of the Observatory (FOTO)

FOTO is a community support group that offers numerous benefits to members and that helps the growth of the Observatory. Become a member and make sure that the stars continue to shine on Griffith Observatory.

Griffith Observatory, 2800 East Observatory Road, Los Angeles, California 90027, USA

[Turn over

Part 4

Questions 21–25

● Read the text and questions below.

● For each question, mark the letter next to the correct answer – **A**, **B**, **C** or **D** – **on your answer sheet**.

Example answer:

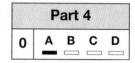

... The first few days after getting home from college were okay but then I began to feel rather bored and lonely. My parents were busy working and most of my friends were either away on holiday or else had holiday jobs. I had tried to get a job myself but without success. I was beginning to wish I had not come home when I saw an advertisement for holiday courses in the local newspaper. For a small fee you could try lots of different activities organized by the town's youth club. Each activity lasted half a day. I had not expected the courses to be very interesting but they were excellent. I also met new people as many of the tourists staying in the town joined in. You could do things like painting, acting, play-writing or computing. I met some students from Bulgaria who invited me to visit Bulgaria next year. You can imagine how excited I am; in fact it was one of the best summer holidays I've ever had!

21 What is the writer trying to do in the text?

A describe a holiday in the country

B explain how she spent a holiday

C describe her new holiday home

D explain why she couldn't go on holiday

22 Why would somebody read the text?

A to find out about holiday courses

B to discover the writer's news

C to make contact with Bulgarian students

D to read about the advertisements

23   How did the writer feel when she arrived home?

A   She was pleased to have time to herself.

B   She felt nervous about being alone.

C   She was delighted to see her friends.

D   She almost regretted coming back.

24   Why is the writer looking forward to next year?

A   There will be new holiday courses.

B   She has found a holiday job.

C   She is planning to go to Bulgaria.

D   Her friends will visit her.

25   Which of these advertisements did the writer see?

A

YOUTH CENTRE

A week's free course on an activity of your own choice. Open to visitors and residents alike. Name your course and you can spend a week enjoying yourself.

B

Sports Centre

Join a holiday course! We are offering half-day courses in a variety of water sports. During the summer holiday period all courses are half price.

C

TOWN HALL

Throughout the summer holiday we are offering cheaper entry to the town's sports and leisure facilities. Special low prices for tourists. Don't miss this opportunity!

D

YOUTH CENTRE

We welcome everyone to join in our holiday programme. A wide range of sports and activities is available on a morning or afternoon timetable.

[Turn over

Part 5

Questions 26–35

● Read the text below and choose the correct word for each space.

● For each question, mark the letter next to the correct word – **A**, **B**, **C** or **D** – **on your answer sheet.**

Example answer:

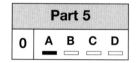

Part 5				
0	A	B	C	D

RAIL DISCO

Every Saturday night at six o'clock during **(0)**............ summer months up to 500 disco fans climb aboard a train in Turin in Italy. They **(26)**............ the next six hours dancing away until the train **(27)**............ a popular disco at one of the towns **(28)**........... the Adriatic coast. The whole trip **(29)**............ eighty dollars, including entrance into the disco.

Italian railways started the idea **(30)**............ a way of trying to reduce the growing numbers of young people **(31)**............ have accidents every weekend as they drive the 400 kilometres to the coast.

Even **(32)**............ the train pulls away from the platform the disco car is crowded with people **(33)**............ all kinds of fashionable clothes. The discos stay open until four in the morning and **(34)**............ at 05.30 the train is ready to begin its journey back to Turin. It will arrive in **(35)**............ for its exhausted passengers to get home for Sunday lunch!

0	**A**	the	**B**	one	**C**	that	**D**	those
26	**A**	go	**B**	spend	**C**	do	**D**	take
27	**A**	comes	**B**	travels	**C**	reaches	**D**	arrives
28	**A**	in	**B**	to	**C**	for	**D**	on
29	**A**	pays	**B**	charges	**C**	makes	**D**	costs
30	**A**	as	**B**	like	**C**	such	**D**	that
31	**A**	what	**B**	these	**C**	who	**D**	they
32	**A**	until	**B**	before	**C**	above	**D**	after
33	**A**	dressing	**B**	having	**C**	wearing	**D**	showing
34	**A**	then	**B**	where	**C**	when	**D**	since
35	**A**	turn	**B**	case	**C**	fact	**D**	time

Writing

Part 1

Questions 1–5

● Here are some sentences about travelling by air.
● For each question, finish the second sentence so that it means the same as the first.
● The second sentence is started for you. **Write only the missing words on your answer sheet.**
● You may use this page for any rough work.

Example: Air travel can be delayed by fog.

Fog .... *can delay air travel.* ....

1   Air travel is faster than any other kind of transport.

   Air travel is the ....

2   You usually have to wait a long time at the airport.

   There are usually ....

3   Plane tickets are also quite expensive.

   You have to pay ....

4   Cheaper tickets are available from some travel agents.

   Some travel agents ....

5   If you are a student you can always get special reduced prices.

   Unless you are a student ....

[Turn over

Part 2

Questions 6–15

● You saw this competition entry form in a local newspaper.
● Look at the form and answer each question.
● **Write your answers on your answer sheet.**
● You may use this page for any rough work.

Gateston Reporter

WIN A LUXURY WEEKEND FOR TWO

Full name: (**6**) ....

Home address: (**7**) ....

Nationality: (**8**)...

Date of birth (day/month/year): (**9**)...

Occupation: (**10**)..

Please write down a country where you would like to spend a weekend:

(**11**)...

Which season of the year would you prefer to go away?

(**12**)...

If you win, who will you take with you?

(**13**)...

How long have you known this person?

(**14**)...

Signature: (**15**)..

Part 3

Question 16

- You have just spent a week at the Europa Park Activity Camp.
- Below is your diary for the week.
- Write a letter to an English-speaking friend telling her/him about what you did on three of the days.
- **Finish the letter on your answer sheet, using about 100 words.**
- You may use this page for any rough work.

Wed.	lake
Thurs.	film
Fri.	competition

Dear

   I have just spent a week at the Europa Park Activity Camp. ....

....

....

....

....

....

....

....

....

....

PAPER 2
Listening Test

(30 minutes + 12 minutes transfer time)

Part 1
Questions 1–7

- There are seven questions in this Part.
- For each question there are four pictures and a short recording.
- You will hear each recording twice.
- For each question, look at the pictures and listen to the recording.
- Choose the correct picture and put a tick (✓) in the box below it.

Example: What time is the match?

A ✓   B ☐   C ☐   D ☐

1 Who is the child going with?

A ☐   B ☐   C ☐   D ☐

2 Where is the library?

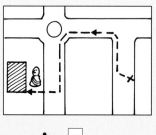   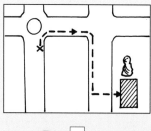   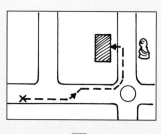   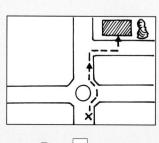

A ☐   B ☐   C ☐   D ☐

3   What's the problem?

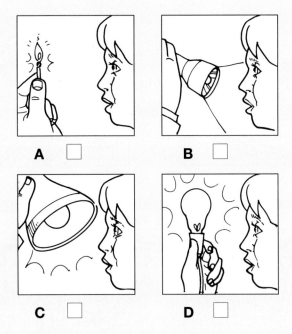

A ☐   B ☐

C ☐   D ☐

4   What is the person holding?

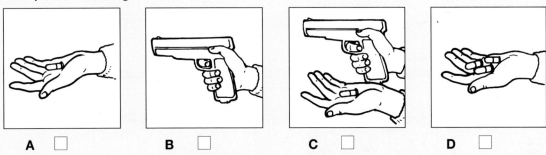

A ☐   B ☐   C ☐   D ☐

5   What happened?

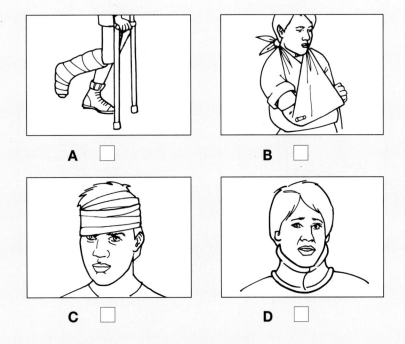

A ☐   B ☐

C ☐   D ☐

[Turn over

6 **What happened?**

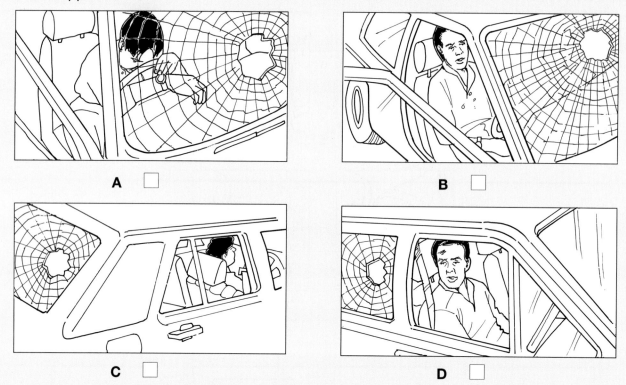

A ☐   B ☐

C ☐   D ☐

7 **What does the customer order?**

A ☐   B ☐

C ☐   D ☐

Part 2

Questions 8–13

● Look at the questions for this Part.
● You will hear the director of a language school talking to some students who have just arrived at the school.
● Put a tick (✓) in the correct box for each question.

8 If your surname begins with J, your family will be in
   A ☐ the school hall.
   B ☐ a room upstairs.
   C ☐ the garden outside.
   D ☐ the dining room.

9 If your surname begins with T, your family will be
   A ☐ in the coach.
   B ☐ by the office.
   C ☐ in the car park.
   D ☐ outside the gate.

10 The party is for students
    A ☐ and their families.
    B ☐ to meet the teachers.
    C ☐ who want to become actors.
    D ☐ who want to study music.

11 Students who need to find a bank should ask
    A ☐ the school director.
    B ☐ at the office.
    C ☐ one of the staff.
    D ☐ their family.

12 Students' fees are due
    A ☐ by next week.
    B ☐ that evening.
    C ☐ in three days.
    D ☐ the following day.

13 The school cook
    A ☐ is a well-known international chef.
    B ☐ offers a wide choice of food daily.
    C ☐ will cook individual meals if asked.
    D ☐ enjoys preparing her own recipes.

[Turn over

Part 3

Questions 14–19

- Look at the notes about Bampton Weekend Festival.
- Some information is missing.
- You will hear a radio announcer talking about the Festival.
- For each question, fill in the missing information in the numbered space.

BAMPTON WEEKEND FESTIVAL

Friday: Parade starts at 19.00 hours

(14).......................... in Alice Park.

Demonstration by **(15)**.......................... on

how to rescue people.

(16).......................... available at gate.

Saturday: Children's Road Race

For children aged 10–14

Entry forms available from **(17)**..........................

All forms must be **(18)**.......................... by an

adult.

Race starts from **(19)**.......................... at

10.00.

Part 4

Questions 20–25

- Look at the six statements for this Part.
- You will hear a conversation over the telephone between a shopkeeper and a woman about a bill.
- Decide if you think each statement is correct or incorrect.
- If you think it is correct, put a tick (✓) in the box under **A** for **YES**. If you think it is not correct, put a tick (✓) in the box under **B** for **NO**.

		A YES	B NO
20	The beds were quite cheap.	☐	☐
21	Mrs Enright usually buys things with her credit card.	☐	☐
22	The clerk found the quantity of money amazing.	☐	☐
23	Mrs Enright has got her receipt.	☐	☐
24	Mrs Enright remains very calm during the conversation.	☐	☐
25	The shopkeeper hopes the police will help with the problem.	☐	☐

Speaking Test

Part 1   **General conversation (2–3 minutes)**

Tasks   Identifying oneself, giving information about people, asking
direct questions.

Sub tasks   Spelling, numbers, responding to questions and information.

Ask each other questions to find out information about personal details, family,
home town, schools, jobs, etc.

Part 2   **Simulated situation (2–3 minutes)**

Tasks   Discussing arrangements, making plans.

You want to have a meal together at a restaurant one evening this week.
You are both quite busy.

Candidate A should look at page 110.

Candidate B should look at page 112.

Talk about the arrangements in your diary, find an evening when you are both free
and then arrange where to meet.

Part 3   **Responding to a visual stimulus**
(5 minutes for Parts 3 and 4 together)

Tasks   Describing people and places, saying where people are and
what they are doing.

Candidate A should look at the picture on page 110, show it to
Candidate B and talk about it.

Candidate B should look at picture 3 on page 111, show it to
Candidate A and talk about it.

Part 4   **General conversation (based on the photographs)**

Tasks   Talking about one's likes and dislikes, expressing opinions.

Talk to each other about the sort of food you enjoy, and the kind of place you like
or don't like to go to when you go out for a meal.

Picture 1

Picture 2

PAPER 1
Reading and Writing Test

(1 hour 30 minutes)

Reading

Part 1

Questions 1–5

- Look at the sign in each question.
- Someone asks you what it means.
- Mark the letter next to the correct explanation – **A**, **B**, **C** or **D** – **on your answer sheet**.

Example:

0

A Come in whenever you like.

B Please ring for an appointment.

C We will call you when we are free.

D Visitors please wait outside.

Example answer:

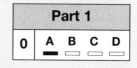

Part 1			
0	**A** B C D

1

A The road in front is closed to traffic.

B The road in front is likely to be busy.

C There are road works further along.

D There is a parking zone further along.

2

Please keep noise
down when lectures
are in progress

A   You should be quiet during teaching hours.

B   You cannot go in once a lecture has begun.

C   Only lecturers are allowed into this building.

D   Please do not leave your lectures early.

3

NIGHT BELL
please ring and wait for reply

A   You cannot get into the hotel after midnight.

B   Please tell the hotel if you are going to be back late.

C   The telephone is at the end of the corridor.

D   Someone will answer your call if you remain here.

4

Please allow at least
half an hour for us
to get your order ready

A   Please collect your order as soon as possible.

B   You may have to wait more than 30 minutes for your order.

C   Your order will be ready in under half an hour.

D   If you wait here we will tell you when your order is ready.

5

PLEASE DO NOT LEAVE
EQUIPMENT OR RUBBISH
IN THIS AREA

A   This area is kept for storing equipment.

B   You are allowed to leave rubbish here.

C   You may not leave any luggage in this area.

D   This area must be kept free of rubbish and equipment.

[Turn over

Part 2

Questions 6–10

- The people below are at an airport and looking for somewhere to eat.
- On the opposite page there are descriptions of eight eating places.
- Decide which place (letters A–H) would be the most suitable for each person (numbers 6–10).
- For each of those numbers mark the correct letter on your answer sheet.

Example answer:

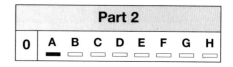

Part 2
0 A B C D E F G H

6

Ken is in a hurry as he is late for his flight. He needs a quick cold drink, however, before he goes to passport control.

7

Jamila is meeting her uncle whose flight arrives at 12.30. She left home early and wants to have a hot meal before he comes, but at the same time be able to see the exit door, as this is his first trip abroad and she is afraid he may get lost.

8

Diane's midday flight has been delayed. The airline has offered to pay for a complete lunch if she sends them her receipt. So she has decided to accept the offer and have a three-course meal.

9

Jorge and his children want a place where they can serve themselves as they each like different things to eat. They don't mind whether they have hot or cold food.

10

Carolyn and her friend have arrived too soon for their morning flight. They got up very early and now they want a hot drink and something sweet to eat with it.

Your Guide to Restaurants and Bars

A

Real Cool

Have you got a sweet tooth? Then this is the place for you. Enjoy one of our special ice-creams served with a chocolate cookie. Lots of different fruit flavours including lemon, banana, strawberry, coconut and orange.
Open 14.00–20.00

B

HEALTHWORKS

This is a colourful kiosk serving a wide variety of drinks. Choose your drink from our fresh fruit and we'll mix it with yoghurt or ice-cream if you want. Or just have a glass of pure, iced juice!
Open 06.30–21.00

C

The Restaurant

The Restaurant is the best place to enjoy a full meal. We offer an international menu with plenty of choice. Choose a starter, followed by a main meal, cheese and dessert all for the price of £17.50.
Open 08.00–15.00

D

Café Bar

Just the place for the younger members of the family! We serve hot dogs, pizzas and hamburgers all cooked on the spot. Try our hot chocolate drinks or have a cup of fresh coffee while you wait. Open 11.30–23.00

E

SEAFOOD & SALAD BAR

Recently opened and already a favourite with all our passengers. Help yourself to our delicious cold fish and salads. There's always something different on the menu. Close to the departure gates to save you time. Our friendly staff will make sure you don't miss your flight!
Open 10.00–21.00

F

Sandwich Side

In a hurry? Then enjoy one of our freshly-made sandwiches. Choose from five different kinds of bread and we'll put whatever you like on top! A complete meal in itself and great value for money!
Open all day

G

C A F É
Rapide

This café is near the Arrivals point. It offers quick, freshly prepared hot dishes. Ideal for people waiting for family or friends or just those who enjoy watching the world go by. Open 06.00–22.00

H

Tea & Coffee House

We serve six different kinds of tea and coffee along with various cakes, biscuits and cookies. You'll find us near the entrance to the shopping galleries. Open 24 hours

[Turn over

Part 3

Questions 11–20

- Look at the statements below about Euro-Youth travel tickets.
- Read the text on the opposite page to decide if each statement is correct or incorrect.
- If it is correct, mark **A on your answer sheet**.
- If it is not correct, mark **B on your answer sheet**.

Example answer:

11   Anyone who is not yet 24 years old can buy a ticket.

12   You are allowed to break your journey wherever you want.

13   You can use your ticket for up to two months at any one time.

14   You have to buy a return ticket.

15   If you travel from London you have to pay extra for sea crossings.

16   You can't buy a ticket without showing your passport.

17   Journeys on certain trains will cost you more.

18   Travel insurance is included in the cost of your ticket.

19   Euro-Youth tickets come with maps and timetables.

20   Euro-Youth tickets offer cheap accommodation in some cities.

A new kind of ticket – a new kind of freedom

Euro-Youth is a new kind of low-cost rail ticket available to young people under 24. It has been designed to take you from London to any one of around 200 selected destinations and let you travel at your own pace.

You can stop off at as many points as you like, for as long as you like within the two month period that your ticket lasts.

The destinations and the routes you can choose from include the European cities that are most often visited by young travellers from around the world: Amsterdam, Paris, Rome, Berlin, Budapest, Venice and many more. And at prices starting as low as 120 dollars all the fares are terrific value.

There is a choice of one-way or return travel tickets, each valid for two months from the date of departure.

Prices include travel from London and ferry crossings from the UK to mainland Europe.

You must have your passport with you when you buy your ticket.

You will have to pay extra on express trains on the Continent, such as the French TGV services, and for sleeping accommodation on other trains.

You are strongly recommended to take out travel insurance for the period of your journey. This is quickly and easily arranged where you can buy this Euro-Youth ticket.

Planning Your Journey

We recommend two publications, in particular, to help you plan your Trans-Euro journey.

The first is a budget guide to Europe, of which there are many available. Particularly good is *Across Europe* by Fay Nuutinen and Bendt Larsen. It covers accommodation, visas, food, sights, customs and even local transport.

The second is Multiplan's *European Timetable*, the only one covering rail and ferry services across the whole of Europe. It is published monthly and also contains plans of major city centres with station locations and detailed notes on how to use the book.

Where To Stay

There is plenty of budget-priced accommodation available in every country in Europe, including Youth Hostels, YMCA Hostels, pensions, 'sleepins' and even convents in Italy. Some people like to save a day by catching the overnight train – but be prepared for fellow travellers to talk into the early hours!

If you're stuck, local tourist offices can usually help to find you a bed.

[Turn over

Part 4

Questions 21–25

● Read the text and questions below.

● For each question, mark the letter next to the correct answer – **A**, **B**, **C** or **D** – on your answer sheet.

Example answer:

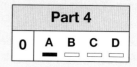

Part 4			
0	A ▬	B ▭	C ▭	D ▭

Anybody running a company knows that a well-planned conference can greatly improve the performance of that business. The main reason for this is that it takes your employees away from the daily work place and offers them somewhere fresh for a short time. However, unless the conference is well thought out it will not have the best results and you will have wasted a great deal of money.

The first step is to find the right place. Can your employees easily reach the conference centre? Is it near a railway station? Is it close to a good, fast road? Has it plenty of suitable parking space? If you are going to choose an hotel, then perhaps the hotel has cheaper rates at weekends or, if it is in a popular tourist area, midweek rates may be cheaper.

Another important requirement is food and drink. Breakfast is a time when people can relax before the day's work begins, but you may not want a long break for lunch in the middle of the day. Buffet lunches are very popular for this reason. Then there is dinner, which most employees consider a reward for a day's hard work!

Whatever your needs, it is essential to think ahead if you want a successful conference.

21 What is the writer trying to do in the text?

  A complain about a bad conference centre

  B describe what makes a good conference centre

  C persuade employers to choose a conference hotel

  D advise employees where to stay for a conference

22 Why would somebody read the text?

  A to find out about organizing conferences

  B to learn how to reward good employees

  C to find out about running a business

  D to learn some details about conference centres

23 What is very important when choosing a conference centre?

   A   cheap food and drink

   B   free car parking

   C   good transport connections

   D   popular tourist areas

24 Why does the writer think a buffet lunch is a good idea?

   A   It's relaxing.

   B   It's quick.

   C   It's cheap.

   D   It's tasty.

25 Which centre would the writer recommend to an employer?

A

☆ STAR ☆
CONFERENCE
CENTRE

Close to airport and golf course.
Choice of conference rooms.
Swimming pool and sauna.
3 full meals a day included in price.

B

✳ Topps *Conference Centre*

- Enjoy beautiful scenery high up in the hills.
- Continental breakfast served in bedroom if wished.
- Minibus service to nearest town.

C

WATT
CONFERENCE
CENTRE

➤   5 minutes from city centre and close to motorway.

➤   Full breakfast, light lunches and exciting dinner menus.

➤   Choice of accommodation to suit your financial needs.

D

Royal Conference Centre

✧   Situated in quiet countryside.

✧   Free car park available for guests.

✧   TV and VHS included in your conference costs as well as three buffet-style meals a day.

[Turn over

Part 5

Questions 26–35

● Read the text below and choose the correct word for each space.

● For each question, mark the letter next to the correct word – **A**, **B**, **C** or **D** – **on your answer sheet**.

Example answer:

Part 5				
0	A	B	C	D

BIRTH OF THE COMPUTER

Most people think of computers as very modern inventions, products of our new technological (**0**)............ . But actually the idea for a computer (**26**)............ worked out over two centuries ago by a man (**27**)............ Charles Babbage.

Babbage was born (**28**)........... 1791 and grew up to be a brilliant mathematician. He drew up plans for several calculating machines (**29**)............ he called 'engines'. But despite the fact that he (**30**)............ building some of these he never finished any of them. Over the years people have argued (**31**)............ his machines would ever work. Recently, however, the Science Museum in London has finished building (**32**)............ engine based on one of Babbage's designs. (**33**)............ has taken six years to complete and more (**34**)............ four thousand parts have been specially made. Whether it works or not, the machine will be on show at a special exhibition in the Science Museum (**35**)............ remind people of Babbage's work.

0	**A** age	**B** year	**C** time	**D** days
26	**A** has	**B** was	**C** had	**D** is
27	**A** known	**B** recognized	**C** written	**D** called
28	**A** on	**B** in	**C** by	**D** for
29	**A** whose	**B** who	**C** these	**D** which
30	**A** wanted	**B** made	**C** started	**D** missed
31	**A** until	**B** whether	**C** while	**D** though
32	**A** some	**B** the	**C** an	**D** that
33	**A** One	**B** He	**C** They	**D** It
34	**A** than	**B** therefore	**C** when	**D** then
35	**A** to	**B** as	**C** for	**D** so

Writing

Part 1

Questions 1–5

● Here are some sentences about crime.

● For each question, finish the second sentence so that it means the same as the first.

● The second sentence is started for you. **Write only the missing words on your answer sheet.**

● You may use this page for any rough work.

Example: Over 300,000 cars are stolen every year.

Thieves ..... *steal over 300,000 cars every year.* .....

1   If possible a car should be kept in a garage at night.

If possible you ....

2   Always take the car keys with you when you park the car.

Don't ....

3   Some stolen cars are driven by young people just for fun.

Young people ....

4   This behaviour is considered to be criminal.

People ....

5   There is great danger in driving too fast.

Driving too fast is ....

[Turn over

Part 2

Questions 6–15

● You want to apply to go on a study holiday.

● Look at the form and answer each question.

● **Write your answers on your answer sheet.**

● You may use this page for any rough work.

INTERNATIONAL STUDY HOLIDAYS

Westhay University
Luxford LX92 1AR
26 July to 15 August

Family name: **(6)** ....

First name(s): **(7)** ....

Full address: **(8)** ....

Date of birth (day/month/year): **(9)** ....

Nationality: **(10)** ....

Occupation: **(11)** ....

Why are you applying for a study holiday?

(12) ....

What languages can you speak?

(13) ....

How will you be travelling?

(14) ....

Signature: **(15)** ....

Part 3

Question 16

● You are on holiday with some friends.

● Write a letter to an English-speaking friend about two things you have done and mention something unpleasant which happened a few days ago.

● **Finish the letter on your answer sheet, using about 100 words.**

● You may use this page for any rough work.

Dear

We arrived here a week ago...

....

....

....

....

....

....

....

....

....

PAPER 2
Listening Test

(30 minutes + 12 minutes transfer time)

Part 1
Questions 1–7

- There are seven questions in this Part.
- For each question there are four pictures and a short recording.
- You will hear each recording twice.
- For each question, look at the pictures and listen to the recording.
- Choose the correct picture and put a tick (✓) in the box below it.

Example: What time is the match?

A ☑   B ☐   C ☐   D ☐

1   What is the man holding?

A ☐   B ☐   C ☐   D ☐

2   Which picture describes the fisherman's day?

A ☐   B ☐   C ☐   D ☐

3   What is happening?

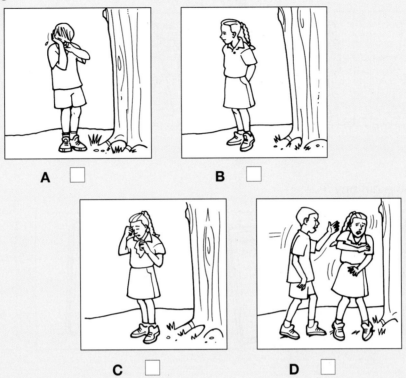

A ☐   B ☐

C ☐   D ☐

4   Who is waiting for Mr Svenson?

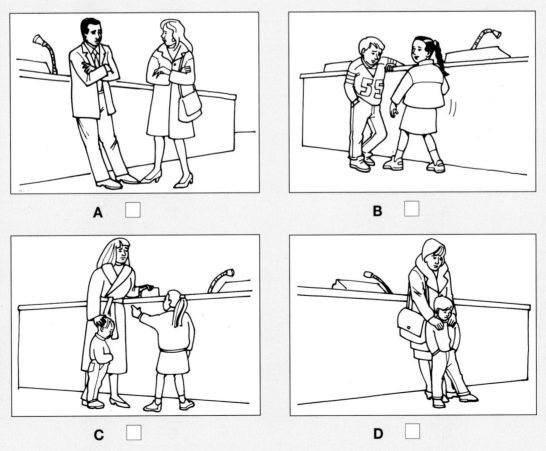

A ☐   B ☐

C ☐   D ☐

[Turn over

5   Which bed does the woman want?

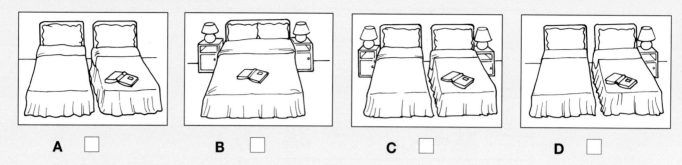

A ☐   B ☐   C ☐   D ☐

6   Which book does the girl buy?

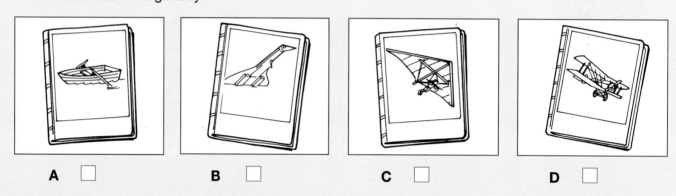

A ☐   B ☐   C ☐   D ☐

7   Where does the man put the playing cards?

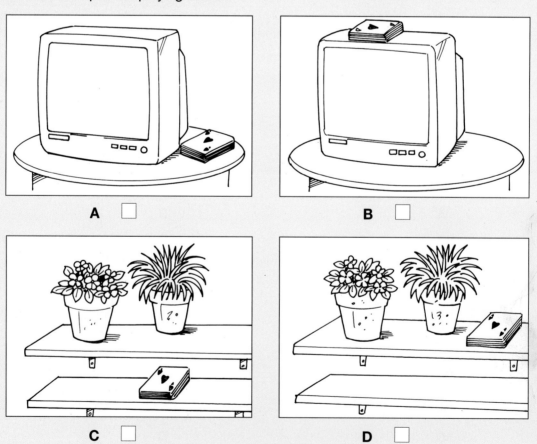

A ☐   B ☐

C ☐   D ☐

Part 2

Questions 8–13

● Look at the questions for this Part.
● You will hear a radio programme about traffic and travel.
● Put a tick (✓) in the correct box for each question.

8 There is a traffic jam

A ☐ on the M3 motorway.

B ☐ in the centre of London.

C ☐ near a motorway exit.

D ☐ on the M4 motorway.

9 London Bridge is

A ☐ closed to traffic.

B ☐ covered with glass.

C ☐ full of lorries.

D ☐ forbidden to walkers.

10 If you're travelling by train

A ☐ everything is normal.

B ☐ you will be delayed.

C ☐ reservations are necessary.

D ☐ check train services.

11 The car park at Manchester airport

A ☐ is closed to the public.

B ☐ has more space than usual.

C ☐ may be completely full.

D ☐ is reserved this weekend.

12 In Birmingham

A ☐ some shops will be closed.

B ☐ you have to travel around by bus.

C ☐ students are organizing a march.

D ☐ police have closed the university.

13 On the M6 motorway

A ☐ it might be very foggy.

B ☐ it is raining hard.

C ☐ there has been an accident.

D ☐ one part has been closed off.

[Turn over

Part 3

Questions 14–19

- Look at the notes about recommended hotels.
- Some information is missing.
- You will hear a radio presenter talking about which hotels to stay at.
- For each question, fill in the missing information in the numbered space.

RECOMMENDED HOTELS

Hotel Flora

All rooms have TV, radio and (14).....................................

Buffet breakfast included in price but not

(15)...............................

(16)............................. **Hotel**

Small, 16 rooms altogether.

Each room has a (17)................................. but breakfast not

included in price.

Hotel Continental

Has a (18)................................. on roof.

Good food, especially desserts.

You pay more for a room facing the (19).................................

Part 4

Questions 20–25

- Look at the six statements for this Part.
- You will hear a conversation between two people who are deciding where to go for the evening.
- Decide if you think each statement is correct or incorrect.
- If you think it is correct, put a tick (✓) in the box under **A** for **YES**. If you think it is not correct, put a tick (✓) in the box under **B** for **NO**.

		A YES	B NO
20	The man is disappointed about missing the play.	☐	☐
21	The woman wishes they had reserved seats.	☐	☐
22	The woman agrees that a concert is a waste of money.	☐	☐
23	The woman likes the idea of visiting his aunt.	☐	☐
24	The woman feels like doing some sport.	☐	☐
25	The man suggests going to the cinema.	☐	☐

Speaking Test

Part 1   **General conversation (2–3 minutes)**

Tasks   Identifying oneself, giving information about people, asking
                 direct questions.

Sub tasks   Spelling, numbers, responding to questions and information.

                 Ask each other questions to find out information about personal details, family,
                 home town, schools, jobs, etc.

Part 2   **Simulated situation (2–3 minutes)**

Tasks   Making plans, stating preferences, agreeing and disagreeing.

                 You have been asked to look after three young children for a day.

                 Look at the picture on page 85.

                 Talk about how you would plan the day and what kind of things
                 you think would entertain them best.

Part 3   **Responding to a visual stimulus**
                 (5 minutes for Parts 3 and 4 together)

Tasks   Describing people and places, saying where people are and
                 what they are doing.

                 Candidate A should look at picture 2 on page 65, show it to
                 Candidate B and talk about it.

                 Candidate B should look at picture 4 on page 111, show it to
                 Candidate A and talk about it.

Part 4   **General conversation (based on the photographs)**

Tasks   Talking about one's likes and dislikes, expressing opinions.

                 Find out about the kinds of things you each enjoy doing in your
                 spare time and when you do them.

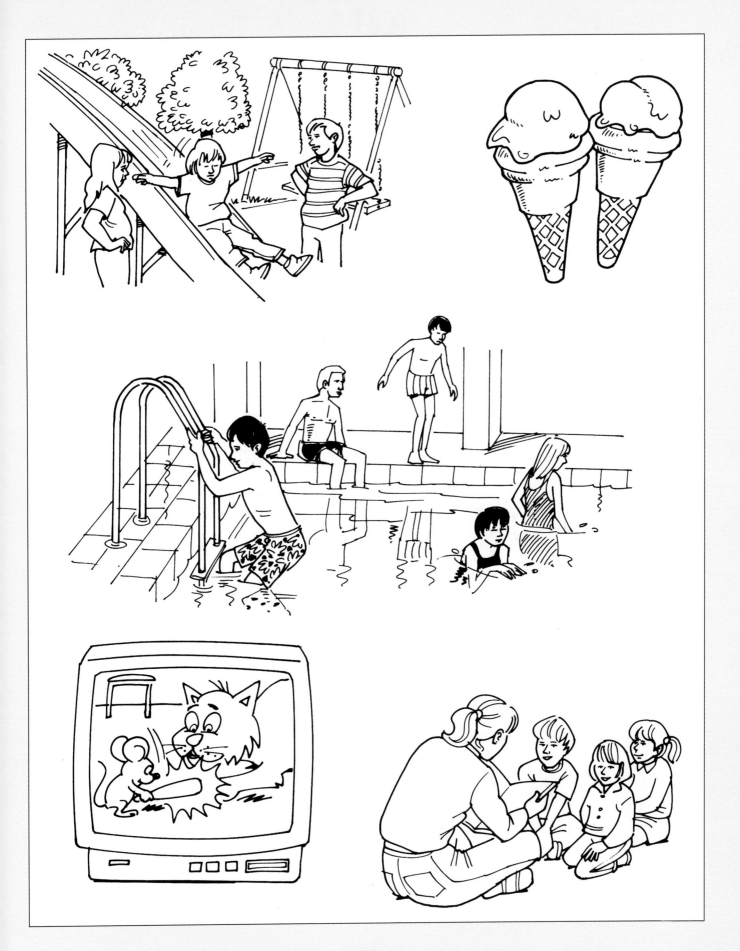

TEST 5

PAPER 1
Reading and Writing Test

(1 hour 30 minutes)

Reading

Part 1

Questions 1–5

- Look at the sign in each question.
- Someone asks you what it means.
- Mark the letter next to the correct explanation – **A**, **B**, **C** or **D** – **on your answer sheet**.

Example:

0

A   Come in whenever you like.

B   Please ring for an appointment.

C   We will call you when we are free.

D   Visitors please wait outside.

Example answer:

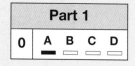

Part 1
0   A   B   C   D

1

A   Don't leave drinks here.

B   Drinks are free here.

C   There are no drinks left.

D   You can buy drinks here.

86

2

A This ground is very soft.

B Don't pick these plants.

C This area is private.

D Don't walk on this area.

3

A You should leave the fish alone.

B These fish can hurt you.

C These fish eat special food.

D You should not fish here.

4

A This shop sells milk drinks.

B You can order milk from here.

C We have no milk left today.

D Milk is not on sale here any more.

5

A Please keep your shopping with you.

B This shop is looking for extra staff.

C Please ask if you need an assistant.

D Please help yourself to what you need.

[Turn over

Part 2

Questions 6–10

- The teachers below are looking for a holiday to suit their students.
- On the opposite page there are descriptions of eight holidays.
- Decide which holiday (**letters A–H**) would be the most suitable for each teacher (**numbers 6–10**).
- For each of those numbers mark the correct letter **on your answer sheet**.

Example answer:

Part 2							
0	A	B	C	D	E	F	G	H

6

Ms Robson's students are studying French and German. She would like to find a holiday which gives them the chance to speak both languages at some point while they're away.

7

Hilary's students are fourteen years old. Some of them learn French, so she wants to find a holiday course which can offer individual language lessons for those who would like to improve their French.

8

Rosie has a small group of students. They all want to sail but unfortunately some of them are unable to swim, although they're keen to learn.

9

Mr Pearson's class has just started to learn German but he wants a holiday which mixes studying the language with plenty of free time to explore the foreign country.

10

John has a class of eleven-year-olds who are crazy about sport. He'd like a course which organizes a complete programme including all kinds of sport, meals and entertainment.

A

Summer Schools in the Czech Republic

Spend a week in a sports centre 15 minutes south of Prague. Each day's programme is organized by our professional trainers for children aged 10–14. Prices include breakfast, lunch and dinner as well as sightseeing trips.

B

SUMMER IN AUSTRIA

We will arrange a programme to suit your students. All our courses take place at the university in Linz. Morning classes are held in German, evening lectures on Austrian history are in English. We offer an exciting programme of evening activities including music, dance and theatre.

C

Greek Sailing Holidays

Arrive by air and then hire one of our new boats with all the latest equipment to sail around the Greek islands. These boats sleep up to twenty students and two teachers. Trained sailing staff are available but you must be able to swim.

D

Summer Courses in Finland

If you love water sports you'll love our one-week sports holiday on the Finnish lakes. There are opportunities to swim, sail and water-ski. Lessons are available if you need them. There is also a chance to learn Finnish at no extra cost! Everyone welcome.

E

TOURING IN FRANCE

Fly to Paris and spend a few days sightseeing in this wonderful city before travelling on to Toulouse. All our tours have a French-speaking guide and accommodation is in comfortable hotels. Prices include breakfast and evening meal only.

F

Holiday Programmes in Germany

We offer morning classes in the German language at all levels from beginners upwards. In the afternoon you are free to join our mountain walks or to go shopping in the nearby town. In the evening we organize a full programme of entertainments. All ages welcome.

G

Swiss Study Tours

Using the excellent Swiss railway system we offer an unusual holiday, sport and study programme. Your hotel is a train: eat and sleep on board and spend each day in a different part of Switzerland. Opportunities to speak French, German and Italian.

H

Summer Schools in France

We offer summer schools for students between the ages of 12 and 16. Live with a French family and choose from a range of different activities including horse-riding, indoor hockey, football, swimming and dry skiing. Private language lessons arranged if requested.

[Turn over

Part 3

Questions 11–20

- Look at the statements below about travelling to Gatwick Airport near London.
- Read the text on the opposite page to decide if each statement is correct or incorrect.
- If it is correct, mark **A on your answer sheet**.
- If it is not correct, mark **B on your answer sheet**.

Example answer:

11   There is a train to Gatwick every quarter of an hour during the day.

12   The rail journey from London Victoria to Gatwick lasts an hour.

13   At Victoria Station there is an escalator on the platform.

14   Refreshments are available in the train's restaurant car.

15   The train stops a short distance outside the airport.

16   Trains leave Gatwick every 30 minutes during the night.

17   You do not need to book a seat on a train.

18   You can use a single ticket for up to a week after you have bought it.

19   Rail tickets across London include the cost of the Underground ticket.

20   You can talk to a telephone operator for more details.

Catch the train to catch the plane.

One of the great advantages of flying from London Gatwick is the ease of getting there on the non-stop GATWICK EXPRESS service from Victoria Station in London. It's reliable, convenient, comfortable and very quick. The journey takes just 30 minutes.

Victoria Station can now boast probably the best City to Airport rail facilities in the world. The new terminal offers an escalator direct to the train-side and also includes in-town check-in facilities, with certain key airlines.

Easy access for taxis, private cars and coaches direct to the front of the GATWICK EXPRESS Terminal makes your departure trouble free.

The fully air-conditioned carriages have plenty of extra luggage space. An 'at your seat' buffet service offers a full range of snacks and drinks.

Gatwick Airport station is directly below the South Terminal. Lifts and escalators link the platforms with the main part of the airport so you can step off the train onto the plane. In fact GATWICK EXPRESS offers everything today's traveller needs to make their journey complete.

FROM GATWICK AIRPORT

GATWICK EXPRESS services leave the airport every 15 minutes during the day, and every 30 minutes early in the morning and late at night.

Journey times are 35 minutes on Sundays.

With this frequent service from early morning until late at night, seat reservations are not required.

Return tickets last for one month, single tickets for three days. For those meeting friends a Day Return fare is available. Please enquire when making your holiday arrangements.

Other rail services to Gatwick

Passengers to the north-west of England and the Midlands can now enjoy high-speed services direct to and from Gatwick Airport, avoiding changing trains in London.

Gatwick Express

Non-stop to Gatwick every 15 minutes

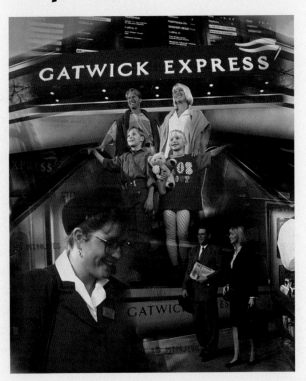

If you are travelling to Gatwick from further afield and your rail journey is across London, you can now use your ticket to transfer by London Underground between your station terminal and Victoria at no extra cost.

For details of these services please ask at your local station.

Further information

Details about the GATWICK EXPRESS are available on a recorded information service, telephone 0171 928 2113.

For enquiries about London Transport cross London Underground connections as well as services from central London to Heathrow Airport, telephone 0171 222 1234 for a recorded information service.

Services may be altered without notice.

It is recommended that journey details are checked near the time of travel.

[Turn over

Part 4

Questions 21–25

● Read the text and questions below.

● For each question, mark the letter next to the correct answer – **A, B, C** or **D** – **on your answer sheet**.

Example answer:

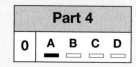

Part 4			
0	A	B	C	D

In the UK we each use about two hundred steel food and drink cans every year. Steel cans are popular because they are convenient, easy to store and unbreakable. But when you have finished with a can what do you do with it? Do you throw it away and forget all about it? Probably! But behind the scenes there are people whose job it is to make sure that the steel is never wasted. In fact, recycling or re-using steel cans is so successful that every day of the year more than five million cans start new lives in new steel products.

After you have thrown away your can, what happens? Well, first of all it is collected by the men who empty your dustbin each week and taken to a tip, together with all the other household rubbish. Then the rubbish is sorted and the steel cans are taken separately to a special factory which turns dirty old cans into high quality steel. It's this steel which may well find its way back into your home in the form of knives and forks, garden equipment and, of course, food and drink cans.

So the next time you open your fizzy drink just remember where your can may have been!

21 What is the writer trying to do in the text?

A advertise canned drinks

B describe the steel industry

C provide some information

D describe rubbish collection

22 Why would somebody read the text?

A to learn about the soft drink industry

B to understand how rubbish is collected

C to find out more about how steel is made

D to discover what happens to old cans

23   How do we know that re-using steel is very successful?

    A   Every person uses 5000 cans a year.

    B   All cans and tins are now made from steel.

    C   Over 5,000,000 cans are recycled daily.

    D   It reduces the amount of waste to collect.

24   What does the writer suggest about our attitude to old cans?

    A   We are not interested what happens to them.

    B   We should be more careful where we throw them.

    C   We could help by sending them to the factory.

    D   We are making things difficult for the dustbin men.

25   Which of the following pictures shows the life of a canned drink?

A
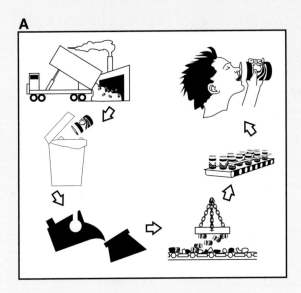

B
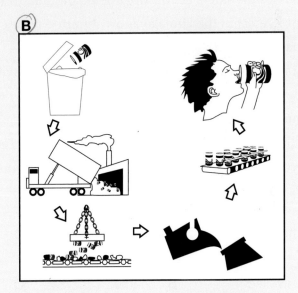

C
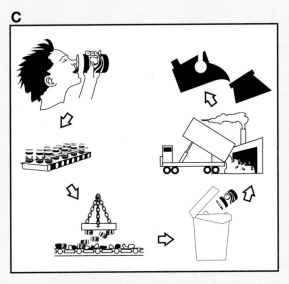

D
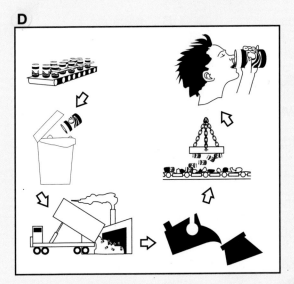

[Turn over

Part 5

Questions 26–35

● Read the text below and choose the correct word for each space.

● For each question, mark the letter next to the correct word – **A**, **B**, **C** or **D** – **on your answer sheet**.

Example answer:

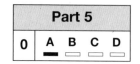

	Part 5			
0	A	B	C	D
	▬	▭	▭	▭

HOLIDAYS THAT DON'T COST THE EARTH

The tourist industry is considered to be (**0**)............ world's largest industry. Before 1950 about 1 million people (**26**)............ abroad each year (**27**)............ by the 1990s the figure had (**28**)............ to over 400 million every year.

(**29**)............ large numbers of tourists, however, are beginning to cause problems. For example, in the Alps the skiers are destroying the mountains (**30**)............ came to enjoy. Even parts of Mount Everest in the Himalayas are reported to be covered (**31**)............ old tins, tents and food that have been (**32**)............ away.

But at a time when we have greater freedom to travel (**33**)............ ever before, more and more people are asking how they can enjoy their holiday (**34**)............ causing problems by spoiling the countryside.

Now there is a new holiday guide called *Holidays That Don't Cost the Earth*. It (**35**)............ you how you can help the tourist industry by asking your travel agent or your tour operator the right questions before you go on holiday.

0	**A** the	**B** a	**C** one	**D** that
26	**A** travelled	**B** came	**C** sailed	**D** were
27	**A** as	**B** because	**C** but	**D** when
28	**A** gone	**B** flown	**C** risen	**D** raised
29	**A** Such	**B** More	**C** Few	**D** So
30	**A** which	**B** you	**C** who	**D** they
31	**A** for	**B** on	**C** with	**D** below
32	**A** put	**B** thrown	**C** given	**D** tidied
33	**A** than	**B** when	**C** then	**D** while
34	**A** outside	**B** instead	**C** beside	**D** without
35	**A** says	**B** offers	**C** tells	**D** gives

Writing

Part 1

Questions 1–5

● Here are some sentences about holiday courses abroad.
● For each question, finish the second sentence so that it means the same as the first.
● The second sentence is started for you. **Write only the missing words on your answer sheet.**
● You may use this page for any rough work.

Example: Courses are organized by Brettan Holidays.

Brettan Holidays ....*organize courses abroad.*............

1 Students must be at least sixteen years old.

   Students have ....

2 Each course lasts two weeks.

   Each course is ....

3 Every tenth student goes free.

   There is no charge ....

4 Students visit museums and galleries.

   There are visits ....

5 Food and transport are included in the price.

   The price ....

[Turn over

Part 2

Questions 6–15

- You have lost your wallet while you were shopping.
- The Lost Property Office has given you this form to fill in.
- Look at the form and answer each question.
- **Write your answers on your answer sheet**.
- You may use this page for any rough work.

LOST PROPERTY OFFICE
Church St.
Camford
CM2 5NT

Family name: **(6)** ....

First name: **(7)** ....

Address: **(8)** ....

What have you lost? **(9)** ....

When did you lose it? **(10)** ....

Please give colour: **(11)** .... and size: **(12)** ....

Please give contents:

(13) ....

Where did you lose your property?

(14) ....

Signature: **(15)** ....

Part 3

Question 16

- You have been staying with an English-speaking friend for a few days.
- Write a letter thanking your friend for your visit and mention three of the things which you particularly enjoyed during your stay.
- **Finish the letter on your answer sheet, using about 100 words**.
- You may use this page for any rough work.

Dear

    I arrived home safely last night after a good journey. ....

....

....

....

....

....

....

....

....

....

PAPER 2
Listening Test

(30 minutes + 12 minutes transfer time)

Part 1

Questions 1–7

- There are seven questions in this Part.
- For each question there are four pictures and a short recording.
- You will hear each recording twice.
- For each question, look at the pictures and listen to the recording.
- Choose the correct picture and put a tick (✓) in the box below it.

Example: What time is the match?

A ☑   B ☐   C ☐   D ☐

1   Where are they meeting?

A ☐   B ☐   C ☐   D ☐

2   What are the shoes like?

   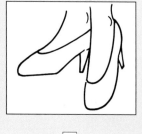   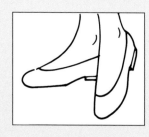   

A ☐   B ☐   C ☐   D ☐

3 What can they see?

A ☐

B ☐

C ☐

D ☐

4 What is he looking for?

A ☐

B ☐

C ☐

D ☐

5 What's the matter?

A ☐

B ☐

C ☐

D ☐

[Turn over

6 What's happening?

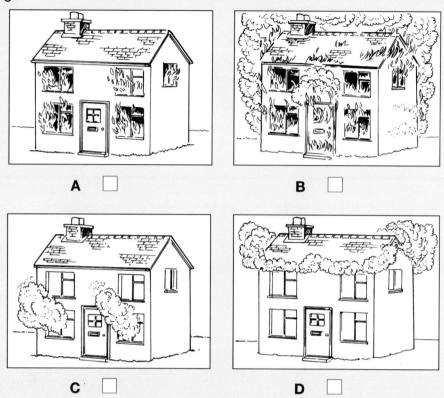

A ☐   **B** ☐

C ☐   **D** ☐

7 What's the complaint?

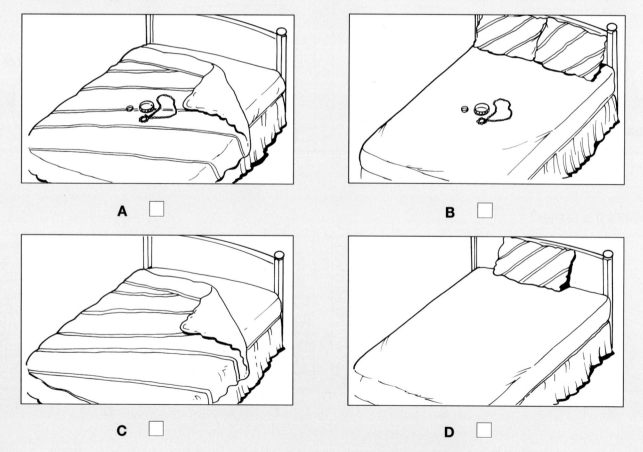

A ☐   **B** ☐

C ☐   **D** ☐

Part 2

Questions 8–13

- Look at the questions for this Part.
- You will hear an announcement on board a ship.
- Put a tick (✓) in the correct box for each question.

8 If you want to keep fit you should

    A ☐ go to C deck.

    B ☐ give your name to Bob.

    C ☐ meet in the games room.

    D ☐ go to the lower deck.

9 The jogging group meets

    A ☐ at 9.00.

    B ☐ in the gym.

    C ☐ on E deck.

    D ☐ in the games room.

10 The morning talk begins with

    A ☐ a film on healthy eating.

    B ☐ you completing your own medical history.

    C ☐ a discussion on staying healthy.

    D ☐ you competing in a health quiz.

11 The weather today

    A ☐ will be changeable.

    B ☐ is the same as yesterday.

    C ☐ remains cool and cloudy.

    D ☐ will be very warm.

12 If you want to see the film you should

    A ☐ avoid being late.

    B ☐ reserve your seat.

    C ☐ queue at 21.00 hours.

    D ☐ buy a ticket.

13 The disco

    A ☐ lasts all night.

    B ☐ has no finishing time.

    C ☐ lasts for three hours.

    D ☐ goes on until 02.00 hours.

[Turn over

Part 3

Questions 14–19

- Look at the notes about a radio competition.
- Some information is missing.
- You will hear a radio presenter talking about the competition.
- For each question, fill in the missing information in the numbered space.

RADIO COMPETITION

Win 2 tickets for a (**14**)...........................

Place: International Football Stadium

Date: (**15**)...........................

Ring (**16**)........................... if you can answer three

questions.

Be ready to give your:

name and address, (**17**)... and

(**18**)...

You are allowed to ring the radio station (**19**)...........................

Part 4

Questions 20–25

- Look at the six statements for this Part.
- You will hear a conversation between a woman called Tanya and a man called Bob who are walking home after a meal in a restaurant.
- Decide if you think each statement is correct or incorrect.
- If you think it is correct, put a tick (✓) in the box under **A** for **YES**. If you think it is not correct, put a tick (✓) in the box under **B** for **NO**.

		A YES	B NO
20	Tanya enjoyed the meal.	☐	☐
21	Bob thinks the meal was good value for money.	☐	☐
22	Tanya thinks the restaurant was good but too expensive.	☐	☐
23	They both agree the music was annoying.	☐	☐
24	Bob agrees that the meal took a long time.	☐	☐
25	Bob is keen to have even more to eat.	☐	☐

Speaking Test

Part 1   **General conversation (2–3 minutes)**

Tasks   Identifying oneself, giving information about people, asking
                    direct questions.

Sub tasks   Spelling, numbers, responding to questions and information.

                    Ask each other questions to find out information about personal details, family,
                    home town, schools, jobs, etc.

Part 2   **Simulated situation (2–3 minutes)**

Tasks   Discussing alternatives, agreeing and disagreeing, making choices.

                    You are studying English in the UK. You have decided to go to an evening class
                    once a week as a way of meeting more people.

                    Look at the picture on page 105.

                    Talk about the things you can do and decide what would be best for you.

Part 3   **Responding to a visual stimulus**
                    (5 minutes for Parts 3 and 4 together)

Tasks   Describing people and places, saying where people are and
                    what they are doing.

                    Candidate A should look at picture 2 on page 45, show it to
                    Candidate B and talk about it.

                    Candidate B should look at picture 2 on page 112, show it to
                    Candidate A and talk about it.

Part 4   **General conversation (based on the photographs)**

Tasks   Talking about one's likes and dislikes, expressing opinions.

                    Talk to each other about whether or not you like shopping and
                    the kind of places you like to do your shopping.

CAMBRIDGE
EXAMINATIONS, CERTIFICATES AND DIPLOMAS
ENGLISH AS A FOREIGN LANGUAGE

University of Cambridge
Local Examinations Syndicate
International   Examinations

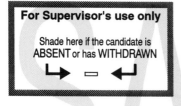

For Supervisor's use only

Shade here if the candidate is
ABSENT or has WITHDRAWN

X

Examination Details	9999/01
Examination Title	Preliminary English Test
Centre/Candidate No.	AA999/9999
Candidate Name	A.N. EXAMPLE

99/D99

• Sign here if the details above are correct

- -

• Tell the Supervisor now if the details above
  are not correct

PET READING ANSWER SHEET

Use a pencil

Mark one letter for each question.

For example:

If you think A is the right answer to the
question, mark your answer sheet like this:

0	A

Change your answer
like this:

Part 1	Part 2	Part 3	Part 4	Part 5
1 A B C D	6 A B C D E F G H	11 A B	21 A B C D	26 A B C D
2 A B C D	7 A B C D E F G H	12 A B	22 A B C D	27 A B C D
3 A B C D	8 A B C D E F G H	13 A B	23 A B C D	28 A B C D
4 A B C D	9 A B C D E F G H	14 A B	24 A B C D	29 A B C D
5 A B C D	10 A B C D E F G H	15 A B	25 A B C D	30 A B C D
		16 A B		31 A B C D
		17 A B		32 A B C D
		18 A B		33 A B C D
		19 A B		34 A B C D
		20 A B		35 A B C D

CAMBRIDGE
EXAMINATIONS, CERTIFICATES & DIPLOMAS
ENGLISH AS A FOREIGN LANGUAGE

University of Cambridge
Local Examinations Syndicate
International Examinations

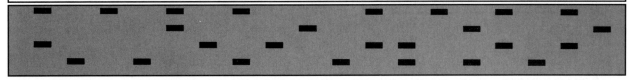

FOR SUPERVISOR'S USE ONLY
Shade here if the candidate
is ABSENT or has WITHDRAWN

X

Examination Details	1999/99	99/D99
Examination Title	P.E.T.	
Centre/Candidate No.	AA999/9999	
Candidate Name	A.N. EXAMPLE	

● Sign here if the details above are correct.

....

● Tell the Supervisor now if the details above
are not correct.

P E T WRITING ANSWER SHEET

Part 1	Do not write here
1	1
2	2
3	3
4	4
5	5

Part 2	Do not write here
6	6
7	7
8	8
9	9
10	10
11	11
12	12
13	13
14	14
15	15

Continue on the other side of this sheet ⟶

Part 3: Write your answer in the box below

Do not write below this line

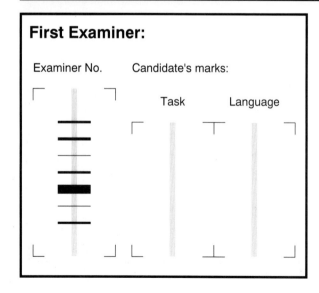

First Examiner:

Examiner No.   Candidate's marks:

                                      Task   Language

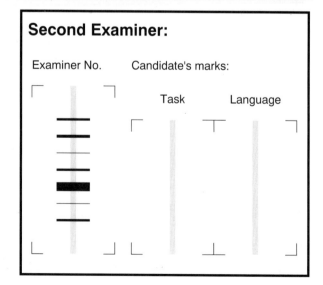

Second Examiner:

Examiner No.   Candidate's marks:

                                      Task   Language

CAMBRIDGE
EXAMINATIONS, CERTIFICATES & DIPLOMAS
ENGLISH AS A FOREIGN LANGUAGE

University of Cambridge
Local Examinations Syndicate
International Examinations

SAMPLE

X

Examination Details

Examination Title

Centre/Candidate No.

Candidate Name

● Sign here if the details above are correct.

● Tell the Supervisor now if the details above are not correct.

PET LISTENING ANSWER SHEET

• You must transfer all your answers from the Listening Question Paper to this answer sheet.

Use a pencil

For Parts 1,2 and 4: Mark one letter for each question.

For example, if you think A is the right answer to the question, mark your answer sheet like this:

Change your answer like this:

0	A ▬

For Part 3: Write your answers in the spaces next to the numbers (14 - 19) like this:

0	*example*	▭ 0 ▭

Part 1		Part 2		Part 3		Do not write here		Part 4	
1	A B C D	**8**	A B C D	**14**		14		**20**	A B
2	A B C D	**9**	A B C D	**15**		15		**21**	A B
3	A B C D	**10**	A B C D	**16**		16		**22**	A B
4	A B C D	**11**	A B C D	**17**		17		**23**	A B
5	A B C D	**12**	A B C D	**18**		18		**24**	A B
6	A B C D	**13**	A B C D	**19**		19		**25**	A B
7	A B C D								

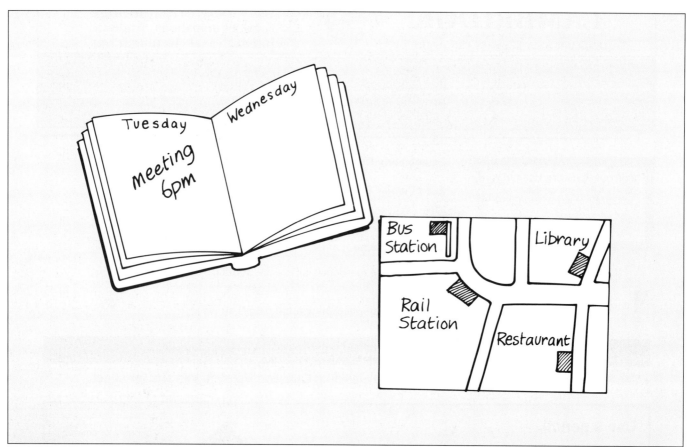

Test 3 Part 2

Test 3 Part 3

Picture 1

Picture 2

Picture 3

Picture 4

111

Picture 1

Picture 2

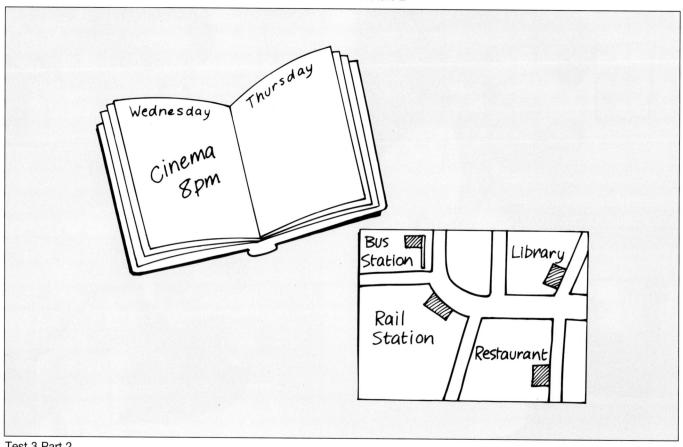

KEY

One mark for each correct answer

TEST 1

Reading

1	C	10	H	19	A	28	A
2	B	11	B	20	A	29	D
3	A	12	B	21	C	30	D
4	C	13	A	22	C	31	B
5	A	14	B	23	A	32	A
6	D	15	B	24	D	33	C
7	E	16	B	25	C	34	B
8	G	17	A	26	C	35	A
9	C	18	B	27	B		

Writing

1 … of choice on the menu.
2 … are special seats for very young children.
3 … day there is a new menu.
4 … includes hot and cold dishes.
5 … can reserve (a) family table(s)/a table for the family.
6 surname/family name
7 first name
8 address in own country
9 nationality

Example

INTERNATIONAL FRIENDSHIP CLUB

22 Palmer Buildings Highampton HG1 6DE

Application form for Membership

Surname: **(6)** *KURTI*

First name: **(7)** *TONY*

Address: **(8)** *Drosselgasse 2, LÜNEBURG GERMANY*

Nationality: **(9)** *German*

Date of birth (day/month/year): **(10)** *5/7/79*

Which languages can you speak?
(11) *English, German*

What are your hobbies?
(12) *Basketball*

Why do you want to join the Club?
(13) *to make more friends*

How long have you been learning English? **(14)** *2 years*

Signature: **(15)** *Tony Kurti*

---

10 day + month + year
11 any language or just mother tongue
12 any suitable hobby, e.g. playing football, cinema
13 any suitable reason, e.g. I want to practise my English, I want a penfriend
14 any suitable length of time, e.g. 6 months
15 NOT printed name
16 There are sample student answers on page 127. The following points should be included:

TASK
• specific suggestions for three things to see and do, NOT just a list
• appropriate length
• appropriate closing formula

LANGUAGE
• appropriate use of structures including tenses
• informal register
• general impression of correct spelling
• range of vocabulary relevant to topic and level
• sentences linked coherently

See page 128 for complete writing information.

Listening

1	C	10	D	18	mountain bike
2	A	11	D	19	blue (and) gold
3	B	12	B	20	B
4	A	13	A	21	A
5	C	14	long dress	22	A
6	D	15	40	23	A
7	D	16	radio cassette (player)	24	A
8	D	17	Walker Street/St.	25	B
9	B				

Speaking

There is a full speaking test on page 126.

Candidates are awarded marks on these four scales:

Fluency
Accuracy and appropriacy of language
Pronunciation
Task achievement

A mark of 0–5 is awarded for each scale ranging from 0 for a candidate who achieves nothing to 5 for a candidate who performs effectively **at this level**. There is no pass mark for each scale. The raw score is weighted so that the speaking test represents 25% of the total score.

TEST 2

Reading

1	A	10	E	19	B	28	D
2	B	11	A	20	B	29	A
3	D	12	A	21	A	30	B
4	C	13	B	22	D	31	C
5	C	14	A	23	B	32	C
6	C	15	B	24	B	33	A
7	F	16	B	25	C	34	B
8	B	17	A	26	B	35	D
9	H	18	B	27	D		

Writing

1 … has two separate swimming pools.
2 … can use/are allowed/permitted to use/can go in.
3 … can go in free/without paying if/don't have to pay/are not charged if you are under 18.
4 … can hire sports equipment.
5 … you fit/healthy.
6 full name
7 address in own country
8 nationality
9 day + month + year
10 male/female
11 any suitable length of time, e.g. 1 year/since I was 10
12 any suitable hobby, e.g. basketball (accept 'I don't have any')
13 any suitable reason, e.g. I want to practise my speaking
14 I don't eat meat (accept No/None/Nothing or a dash)
15 NOT printed name
16 There is a sample student answer on page 127.
   TASK
   clear mention of the three points: new house, neighbours and the area

See page 128 for complete writing information.

Listening

1	A	14	staff room
2	A	15	police
3	D	16	clock
4	D	17	painting
5	C	18	(eight/8) glasses
6	B	19	exam(ination) papers
7	A	20	A
8	D	21	B
9	B	22	B
10	C	23	A
11	B	24	A
12	B	25	B
13	D		

Speaking

See page 113 for marking information.

TEST 3

Reading

1	D	10	G	19	A	28	D
2	D	11	B	20	B	29	D
3	C	12	A	21	B	30	A
4	C	13	B	22	B	31	C
5	A	14	B	23	D	32	B
6	E	15	A	24	C	33	C
7	F	16	B	25	D	34	A
8	B	17	A	26	B	35	D
9	H	18	B	27	C		

Writing

1 … fastest kind of transport.
2 … long waits at the airport/long waiting times.
3 … quite a lot for (a) plane ticket(s).
4 … offer/have/sell cheaper tickets; make cheaper tickets available.
5 … you can't always get special reduced prices.
6 full name
7 address in own country
8 nationality
9 day + month + year
10 any suitable occupation, e.g. student, nurse, housewife
11 one country only EXCLUDING OWN COUNTRY
12 spring/summer/autumn/winter/rainy/dry/hot; NOT A MONTH
13 any person, e.g. my sister etc. Accept proper name, e.g. Petra
14 any suitable length of time, e.g. 2 years
15 NOT printed name
16 There is a sample student answer on page 128.
   TASK
   • reference to three activities (not necessarily those illustrated/mentioned)
   • attempt to elaborate as opposed to mere listing

See page 128 for complete writing information.

Listening

1	D	14	concert
2	A	15	emergency services
3	C	16	tickets
4	A	17	festival office
5	B	18	signed
6	B	19	Town Hall Square
7	C	20	B
8	D	21	A
9	C	22	A
10	B	23	B
11	D	24	B
12	A	25	B
13	C		

Speaking

See page 113 for marking information.

TEST 4

Reading

1	B	10	H	19	B	28	B
2	A	11	A	20	B	29	D
3	D	12	A	21	B	30	C
4	B	13	A	22	D	31	B
5	D	14	B	23	C	32	C
6	B	15	B	24	B	33	D
7	G	16	A	25	C	34	A
8	C	17	A	26	B	35	A
9	E	18	B	27	D		

Writing

1 … should/ought to keep a/your car in a garage at night.
2 … leave the/your car keys in the car when you park.
   forget to take the/your car keys with you when you park.
3 … drive (some) stolen cars (just) for fun.
4 … consider this to be criminal behaviour/behaviour to be criminal.
5 … very dangerous/full of danger.
6 family name/surname
7 first name
8 address including country
9 day + month + year
10 nationality
11 any suitable occupation, e.g. student, housewife
12 any suitable reason, e.g. to meet people from other countries
13 any language
14 any suitable answer, e.g. by car/with my friend
15 NOT printed name
16 There is a sample student answer on page 128.
   TASK
   • clear mention of two holiday activities – not necessarily with reference to the picture stimulus
   • mention of something **unpleasant**, e.g. minor accident

See page 128 for complete writing information.

Listening

1	A	14	bathroom
2	D	15	lunch and dinner/other meals
3	C	16	Gold Cross
4	C	17	shower
5	D	18	(swimming)(heated) pool
6	B	19	mountains
7	C	20	A
8	D	21	A
9	B	22	B
10	D	23	B
11	C	24	A
12	C	25	B
13	A		

Speaking

See page 113 for marking information.

TEST 5

Reading

1	D	10	A	19	A	28	C
2	D	11	A	20	B	29	A
3	A	12	B	21	C	30	D
4	D	13	A	22	D	31	C
5	C	14	B	23	C	32	B
6	G	15	B	24	A	33	A
7	H	16	B	25	B	34	D
8	D	17	A	26	A	35	C
9	F	18	B	27	C		

Writing

1 … to be (at least) sixteen years old.
2 … two weeks long/in length/for two weeks.
3 … for every tenth student.
4 … to museums and galleries for/by the students.
5 … includes food and transport.
6 family name/surname
7 first name
8 address to include town/city NOT just street or apartment
9 wallet
10 day + month + year
11 any suitable colour, e.g. brown
12 any suitable size, e.g. small OR 20 cm x 20 cm
13 any suitable contents, e.g. money, credit cards etc.
14 any suitable place, e.g. on the bus, in the supermarket
15 NOT printed name
16 There is a sample student answer on page 128.
   TASK
   • clear expression of thanks/gratitude
   • mention of three positive aspects of the visit

See page 128 for complete marking information.

Listening

1	B	14	laser show
2	C	15	April 23(rd) or 23/4
3	C	16	0151 66438
4	A	17	telephone number/tel. no. } any
5	D	18	age } order
6	D	19	once/one time
7	A	20	A
8	D	21	B
9	D	22	B
10	B	23	B
11	D	24	A
12	A	25	A
13	B		

Speaking

See page 113 for marking information.

TAPESCRIPTS

TEST 1

P = presenter
V = voice

P   *This is Preliminary Test One. There are four Parts to the Test. You will hear each recording twice. During the Test there will be a pause before each Part to allow you to look through the questions, and other pauses to let you think about your answers. You should write your answers on the question paper. You will have twelve minutes at the end to transfer your answers to the separate answer sheet.*

Part One
There are seven questions in this Part. For each question, there are four pictures and a short recording. You will hear each recording twice. For each question, look at the pictures and listen to the recording. Choose the correct picture and put a tick in the box below it.

Before we start, here is an example.

What time is the match?

V1   Are you going to watch the match on television tonight?
V2   I don't know. What time's it on?
V1   Ten past eight.

P   *The woman says the match starts at ten past eight. The first picture is correct and the tick has been put in the box under the picture.*

Now we are ready to start. Here is a short recording for the first four pictures. Don't forget to put a tick in one of the boxes! Listen carefully…

One   *Where is Maria?*

V1   Have you seen Maria anywhere?
V2   She's in the garden, reading.
V1   Oh, is Anna with her?
V2   No, she's alone.

P   **Two**   *What are they going to eat?*

V1   Gosh, I'm hungry. What's for supper? I hope you've made plenty of chips.
V2   I haven't, actually. I've just made a large salad, but there's a loaf of fresh bread if you want it.

P   **Three**   *Where are the two friends going to meet?*

V1   Are you coming to the meeting tonight?
V2   Yes. What time does it start?
V1   Eight o'clock. I'll meet you outside the gate.
V2   OK.

P   **Four**   *Which picture is their mother?*

V1   Look at this picture of Mum when she was a girl.
V2   Let's see. Is that her in those glasses?
V1   No, not that one. This is her with all that long curly hair and amazingly short skirt.
V2   Wow!

P   **Five**   *What has happened to the boy's bike?*

V1   I'm not going out this evening after all.
V2   I thought you and Yann were going for a bike ride.
V1   We were, but the front wheel of my bike's bent and I haven't been able to fix it.

P   **Six**   *Where did the man spend his holiday?*

V1   Did you have a good holiday?
V2   Yes, great. Instead of our usual two weeks camping by the sea, we rented a cottage in the mountains. The scenery was wonderful and we went for long walks every day without seeing a single person.

P   **Seven**   *What's the problem?*

V1   (scream)
V2   What's the matter?
V1   There's a huge bee!
V2   It won't hurt you. It's more interested in the jar of jam than you!

P   *That is the end of Part One. You now have half a minute to check your answers. We will tell you when Part Two begins.*

Now turn to Part Two, questions 8–13. Look at the questions for this Part. You will hear a woman giving details about the week's activities at a summer camp. Put a tick in the correct box for each question. At the end, the recording is repeated. Now we are ready to start. Listen carefully…

V   … please can we have some quiet. The longer you take to stop talking, the longer it'll be before you can all go. I know you're excited, but if you don't listen you won't know where to go. Right. Now the first day of the course is always a bit confusing, so listen carefully and then you'll know what to do.

Those of you doing rock climbing put your hands up. OK. You had better go now because Guy is waiting for you. Off you go to the gym. That's past the swimming pool and the car park. You can't miss it – it's a great big yellow building. Oh, just a minute. At the end of the morning, that's at midday, make sure you come back here to the grass tennis courts and your group leader will take you off to lunch which is served at 12.30. Don't be late because the afternoon courses start at 13.30.

Now the group doing horse riding. You have to wait at the main gates for the bus. Make sure you're wearing either

116

riding boots or strong shoes – not trainers. The bus will bring you back for lunch but it will stop on the road outside the reception area, so you will just have to walk the few metres to the tennis courts and your group leader will meet you there.

And finally, those of you doing disco dancing. Your class meets in the drama hall. That's the building you can see through the trees on your right. Go straight in, through the music studio, past the practice rooms and up the stairs. You must remember to take a towel because you have showers over there before meeting up for lunch.

A couple more things before you all disappear. Please make sure that you tell your teachers as soon as possible if you want to change your course. Then they can fill in another form for you. Don't just go off to a new class without saying anything or we shall start looking for you and that wastes everybody's time.

Oh yes, one very important thing, food. When it's fine, we shall eat outside and that means you have to collect your own picnic lunch from the dining room. Don't expect your group leader to collect it for you. You'll find a picnic box with your name on it. Then in the evening we organize a barbecue and each group takes it in turn to cook for the whole camp so…

P *Now listen again.*

That is the end of Part Two. You now have a minute to check your answers. We will tell you when Part Three begins.

Now turn to Part Three, questions 14–19. Look at the notes about some things which are being advertised for sale on a radio programme. Some information is missing. You will hear different people talking about what they want to sell. For each question, fill in the missing information in the numbered space. At the end, the recording is repeated.

Now we are ready to start. Listen carefully…

V1 … Hi there everyone and it's time again for Radio 749 Shop Window. And our number, if you don't already know it, is double three – five – seven – eight. If you have anything to sell, then ring in during the programme and we'll see what we can do to help you. And our first caller is on the line. Isabel, hi there, Isabel! And what have you got to sell?

V2 Oh, hello, Rod. Um I've got a dress. A long dress, actually, in pale pink silk. I've only worn it once and it seems a pity to just leave it in the wardrobe. It originally cost £500 but I'm only asking £200 for it. It's size 40 and if people would like to ring me they're welcome to come and try it on.

V1 And your number, Isabel?

V2 Oh, right. 491268.

V1 Many thanks and on to our next caller who is…?

V3 Tony Banks. I've got a radio cassette player I want to sell. It's only a few months old and it's a really good one. They cost over a hundred pounds in the shops. This one's red and I want £65 for it, but I'm open to offers! I'm not on the phone but you can call round any day after six o'clock. And I live at 21 Walker Street. So don't all rush!

V1 Thank you, Tony, and our third caller is on the line and it's Ted Jones. Right, Ted, what are you wanting to sell?

V4 Well, I've got a real bargain. It's a mountain bike – in brilliant condition, blue and gold – and it's hardly been ridden. It'd cost a fortune to buy new and I'm willing to sell it for £340 cash. Ring me on my work number – that's 73155 any time and you can ride it home. But you'll have to ring straight away if you're interested because…

P *Now listen again.*

That is the end of Part Three. You now have a minute to check your answers. We will tell you when Part Four begins.

Now turn to Part Four, questions 20–25. Look at the six statements for this Part. You will hear a conversation between a garage owner and a woman who recently bought a car from him. Decide if you think each statement is correct or incorrect. If you think it is correct, put a tick in the box under A for YES. If you think it is not correct, put a tick in the box under B for NO. At the end, the recording is repeated.

Now we are ready to start. Listen carefully…

V1 Hello there, Mrs Murray.

V2 Ah, good morning, Mr. Horner. I was hoping to see you.

V1 Always happy to see a good customer. What can I do for you?

V2 Well, I'm not very happy with this new car which I bought last month.

V1 We've never had any complaints before about that model. It's one of the best cars on the road. I drive one myself, you know. Never had anything wrong with it.

V2 Well, I'm having problems trying to start mine. Every morning it's the same thing. And I've been late for work because of it.

V1 Leaving it out at night are you, eh? I expect it's getting damp.

V2 No, I never leave it out at night. I put it away in the garage as soon as I get home from work. It's really annoying. There must be something wrong with the engine.

V1 Well, I suppose we'd better have a look at it for you. Bring it in next week and…

V2 I'd like you to look at it as soon as possible, Mr Horner. I didn't expect all this inconvenience with a new car.

V1 Well, we're very busy this week. Why don't you bring it in early tomorrow morning and I'll get one of the lads to look at it? But you'll need to leave it all day because he'll have to drive it around a bit.

V2 In that case, can you lend me a car for the day, please? I can't manage all day without transport.

V1 Well, I don't know. We only lend out cars for the day to customers who are having theirs repaired.

V2 But I am!

V1 We don't know there's anything wrong with it yet.

V2 But I wouldn't be bringing it in if it was perfectly all right, would I?!

V1 Look, I can't make any promises, Mrs Murray. Come and have a word with me tomorrow morning and I'll see what can be done.

V2 Very well, Mr Horner.

117

P Now listen again.

That is the end of Part Four. You now have twelve minutes to check and transfer your answers to the answer sheet.

That is the end of the Test.

TEST 2

P *This is Preliminary Test Two. There are four Parts to the Test. You will hear each recording twice. During the Test there will be a pause before each Part to allow you to look through the questions, and other pauses to let you think about your answers. You should write your answers on the question paper. You will have twelve minutes at the end to transfer your answers to the separate answer sheet.*

Part One
There are seven questions in this Part. For each question, there are four pictures and a short recording. You will hear each recording twice. For each question, look at the pictures and listen to the recording. Choose the correct picture and put a tick in the box below it.

Before we start, here is an example.
What time is the match?

V1 Are you going to watch the match on television tonight?
V2 I don't know. What time's it on?
V1 Ten past eight.

P *The woman says the match starts at ten past eight. The first picture is correct and the tick has been put in the box under the picture.*

Now we are ready to start. Here is a short recording for the first four pictures.

Don't forget to put a tick in one of the boxes! Listen carefully…

One *What happened at the airport?*

V1 Did you hear about that robbery at the airport?
V2 No. What happened?
V1 Some thieves managed to steal people's luggage while it was being loaded onto a plane in broad daylight!

P **Two** *What does the flag look like?*

V1 Which country does that flag belong to?
V2 I can't see it properly. What's it like?
V1 It's black with a line down the middle and a star either side of the line.
V2 I've no idea. I don't recognize it at all.

P **Three** *What are they watching?*

V1 Oh look, aren't they sweet! Can you see those two playing with a ball?
V2 I wouldn't call lions sweet and I'm glad I'm not that ball.

P **Four** *What did she buy?*

V1 What did you buy then? Did you get the skirt you wanted?
V2 No, I couldn't find what I wanted but I spent too much, as usual. Anyway, I got a lovely shirt, a pair of jeans and – wait for it – a hat!
V1 A hat? I thought you hated hats!

P **Five** *Where's the flour?*

V1 Pass me the flour, please.
V2 Which tin is it in?
V1 The one at the end of the shelf. It's slightly smaller than the others.
V2 Oh, right.

P **Six** *What's the weather going to be like?*

V1 Do you know what the weather's going to be like tomorrow? We're hoping to have a picnic by the river.
V2 Then take your umbrella because it's sunshine and showers.
V1 Oh no. Last time we went, the weather was perfect.

P **Seven** *What happened?*

V Police are looking for the driver of a lorry which hit a parked car at the corner of Station Road early today. The driver of the lorry failed to stop and two passengers in the car were badly injured. Anyone who saw the accident is…

P *That is the end of Part One. You now have half a minute to check your answers. We will tell you when Part Two begins.*

Now turn to Part Two, questions 8–13. Look at the questions for this Part.

You will hear a radio programme which recommends somewhere to stay for a short holiday. Put a tick in the correct box for each question. At the end, the recording is repeated.

Now we are ready to start. Listen carefully…

V1 … and at this point in the programme, we come to our recommendation of the week. If you are looking for a weekend break, why not pay a visit to Ternmouth? I know that for most of us Ternmouth is a large city with heavy industry, the second biggest port in the country and hardly the place you would think of going to for a quiet weekend break. But hidden away are all kinds of exciting places and here's Julia to tell us more.

V2 Most of us know Ternmouth as the place we drive through to catch the ferry when we're going on holiday and we've probably never thought of stopping there. Well, a few minutes from the ferry terminal is the main shopping street. A walk along this street and you come across all kinds of inexpensive shops: clothes boutiques, craft shops, bookshops, specialist food shops and more.

And if you're looking for somewhere to eat, you couldn't wish for more choice. Some of the fish restaurants are the best I've ever eaten in. The menus are clearly advertised outside each restaurant so you know exactly what you're paying for. The fish is fresh, usually caught that same day.

Some of the restaurants are built into the sea wall and overlook the harbour. You will find they serve drinks and hot meals throughout the day.

So where to stay? There are plenty of hotels and they vary in price. If you're looking for just bed and breakfast, I'd recommend going for one of the small, cheaper hotels in the old town. If you stay on a bed and breakfast basis – most of them don't have a restaurant anyway – then you can take all your other meals in different places in town, which is great fun.

If you're looking for something with a little more luxury, then I'd suggest one of the cliff-top hotels. High up and hidden behind trees are two or three very grand hotels offering all the comforts you would expect, with their own swimming pools as well. However, there are no buses to this area so you'll need your own transport from the city centre. Parking is no problem and in the busy season some of the hotels run their own taxi service.

Now, for those of you interested in visiting Ternmouth, I'd recommend ringing the tourist office for further details. They'll also send you up-to-date information. Have a pencil ready and I'll give you the phone number; double two–zero–eight–one–six.

We'll give you the number again at the end of the programme, but if you do decide to spend a…

P *Now listen again.*

That is the end of Part Two. You now have a minute to check your answers. We will tell you when Part Three begins.

Now turn to Part Three, questions 14–19. Look at the notes about stolen property. Some information is missing. You will hear a college director talking to some students about what has been stolen. For each question, fill in the missing information in the numbered space. At the end, the recording is repeated.

Now we are ready to start. Listen carefully…

V Good morning, everyone. Thank you for coming along. I'm afraid there is a serious matter which I am hoping we can clear up as soon as possible. Last night, someone broke into the staff room and a number of things are missing. I have already spoken to the police and I trust things will go no further. The police believe that whoever is responsible for the theft is probably a member of this college.

Now, the things that are missing. First of all, a valuable clock which was presented to the college over a hundred years ago has disappeared. The clock cannot easily be sold as it has the name of the college on the front and would immediately be recognized. A painting of the college by Arnolfini has also been stolen, and again this would be easily recognized as it shows the main college buildings.

Now, whoever took these objects also broke open the cupboard in the staff room and took some antique glasses, eight altogether. These were given to the college many years ago by another director. They could easily get broken

and although they are insured they could not be replaced. I'm glad to say the bottles of drink were not removed.

Not surprisingly, both the TV and video recorder have been taken. But perhaps most worrying of all, is the fact that the end-of-term examination papers have been stolen from the filing cabinet. If these papers cannot be marked, everyone in the college will suffer. Without these papers there can be no results, and without results there can be no jobs for those of you who have been offered jobs which depend on these results. Now if you can help, if you have seen or heard anything which…

P *Now listen again.*

That is the end of Part Three. You now have a minute to check your answers. We will tell you when Part Four begins.

Now turn to Part Four, questions 20–25. Look at the six statements for this Part. You will hear a conversation between a woman called Sally and a man called Karl who are making plans for a party. Decide if you think each statement is correct or incorrect. If you think it is correct, put a tick in the box under A for YES. If you think it is not correct, put a tick in the box under B for NO. At the end, the recording is repeated.

Now we are ready to start. Listen carefully…

V1 Karl, have you got the list of people we're inviting to the party?

V2 Well, it's the usual crowd plus the couple from next door.

V1 Oh no, not them, they're so boring.

V2 Look, Sally, I know. But they'll guess we're having a party because of the noise and in any case we asked them last time.

V1 Oh, all right. What about food and drink then?

V2 Well, it's the usual arrangement. We'll provide the food and everyone will bring along something to drink.

V1 Sounds good to me. What're we eating?

V2 I don't know. I've been so busy I haven't done anything about it yet.

V1 How about salads – you know different sorts of salads?

V2 We did that last time. I think we should do something different this time.

V1 What about that chicken thing we had when we were on holiday?

V2 You mean that chicken and rice with strawberries and grapes and stuff?

V1 Yeah, I can't remember what it was called. It was really nice!

V2 I didn't like it that much. I don't like chicken with things like fruit. No, I'll think about it later today and look up a few recipes.

V1 OK. Music? Shall I ask Yusef to bring some of his cassettes?

V2 Well, how about getting a video for a change?

V1 A video? You mean all sit round and watch a video?

V2 Why not? We could hire a really good movie.

V1 Well, I don't see any point in having a party in that case!

V2 All right. It was just an idea but it doesn't matter. Forget it.

V1 Honestly, Karl, you do have some funny ideas at times!

119

P Now listen again.

That is the end of Part Four. You now have twelve minutes to check and transfer your answers to the answer sheet.

That is the end of the Test.

TEST 3

P This is Preliminary Test Three. There are four Parts to the Test. You will hear each recording twice. During the Test there will be a pause before each Part to allow you to look through the questions, and other pauses to let you think about your answers. You should write your answers on the question paper. You will have twelve minutes at the end to transfer your answers to the separate answer sheet.

Part One
There are seven questions in this Part. For each question there are four pictures and a short recording. You will hear each recording twice. For each question, look at the pictures and listen to the recording. Choose the correct picture and put a tick in the box below it.

Before we start, here is an example.

What time is the match?

V1 Are you going to watch the match on television tonight?
V2 I don't know. What time's it on?
V1 Ten past eight.

P The woman says the match starts at ten past eight. The first picture is correct and the tick has been put in the box under the picture.

Now we are ready to start. Here is a short recording for the first four pictures.

Don't forget to put a tick in one of the boxes! Listen carefully…

One Who is the child going with?

V1 Hi! Where're you going?
V2 The swimming pool. Do you want to come?
V1 Who're you going with?
V2 My parents. They're really good swimmers.

P **Two** Where is the library?

V1 Excuse me, could you tell me where the library is, please?
V2 Um, let me think. Right. You're not too far away. Cross over here and turn left, then left again at the roundabout, and you'll see a large sculpture on the pavement. That's just in front of the library.
V1 Thanks.

P **Three** What's the problem?

V1 Hey, don't do that!
V2 What?
V1 Shine that lamp in my eyes. The light's really bright.
V2 Sorry.

P **Four** What is the person holding?

V1 What're you playing with?
V2 It's an old bullet.
V1 A bullet!
V2 It's all right, it's not live. My grandfather gave it to me years ago but he didn't give me his gun!

P **Five** What happened?

V1 Have you seen Rob? He broke his arm at the weekend.
V2 Oh no! I'd heard he'd hurt himself but I thought it was just a few cuts and nothing too serious.

P **Six** What happened?

V1 How on earth did that happen? Did you hit something?
V2 No. I was driving along when a stone suddenly hit the windscreen.
V1 How awful. What a good job it didn't hit you!

P **Seven** What does the customer order?

V1 What can I get you?
V2 A mineral water, please.
V1 With ice?
V2 No, thanks, without. Oh, and a dish of peanuts.
V1 Certainly.

P That is the end of Part One. You now have half a minute to check your answers. We will tell you when Part Two begins.

Now turn to Part Two, questions 8–13. Look at the questions for this Part.

You will hear the director of a language school talking to some students who have just arrived at the school. Put a tick in the correct box for each question. At the end, the recording is repeated.

Now we are ready to start. Listen carefully…

V Good afternoon, everyone. My name's Richard Parry and I'm the school director. I do hope you have all had a good journey, although I'm sure you must be feeling rather tired. No doubt you are looking forward to meeting the families you're going to be staying with during the next month. Now, please listen carefully to the following arrangements as the various families are waiting in groups to meet you.

If your surname – your family name that is – begins with the letter A to F, your host family will be waiting for you in this hall. At the end of the meeting, *you* should wait behind in here. Now, for those of you whose name begins with G to L – *you* should go downstairs, not upstairs, but downstairs to the dining room. When you get there, make sure you go to the far end of the room by the drinks machine. That's important as people whose names begin with a letter from M to R should also go downstairs and wait at the opposite end of the dining room near the doors into the garden. And the final group – those of you with names from S to Z, must go out of this hall, past the office to the car park – (where the coach stopped when you arrived) all right? – out to where the cars are parked by the main gate and *your* families will be waiting there.

Just a few more things before you go, please. Tomorrow

120

night there will be an introductory party with your teachers. We hope you will all come. There'll be food and drink, games and music and, if you play a musical instrument, let us know as we need some more musicians! Or, if you would like to join in the entertainment – perhaps you sing or dance – come along early and help the teachers prepare the programme.

During the day, your family will show you around the town. They'll also tell you which bus to catch so you can get to school each day and they'll answer all your questions about where things are, like the banks, the shops, the post office and so on. But my office staff are always willing to help with difficulties over travel or visas, for example.

If you haven't paid your school fees – and some of you haven't – will you please do so by this time next week. I realize some of you may need to change money and will need time to go to the bank, which is why we give you seven days. If there are any problems then please come and see me.

And finally, food. Very important, as I'm sure you'll agree. We do offer a small choice at lunch time. All your other meals are taken with your family. However, if you have a special request, within reason, and you tell our chef what it is, she will do her best to prepare it for you. You may need to give her the recipe, but she's an excellent cook and in the past has cooked all kinds of different food. Now if you have any questions, then…

P   *Now listen again.*

That is the end of Part Two. You now have a minute to check your answers. We will tell you when Part Three begins.

Now turn to Part Three, questions 14–19. Look at the notes about the Bampton Weekend Festival. Some information is missing. You will hear a radio announcer talking about the Festival. For each question, fill in the missing information in the numbered space. At the end, the recording is repeated.

Now we are ready to start. Listen carefully…

V1   … and today sees the start of the Bampton Weekend Festival. Non-stop fun and entertainment for the whole family from Friday evening through to late night Sunday. And here's Rebecca with the programme details, so have a pencil ready.

V2   There's so much happening this weekend that I'm afraid I can't give you details about everything. However, I'll tell you about some of the main things and you can pick up a detailed programme from the Festival Office in town. The weekend starts with a parade this evening at nineteen hundred hours leaving from the Town Hall steps and finishing up at the sports stadium. For those of you who enjoy good music, there's a concert in Alice Park at twenty thirty hours given by the Bampton Youth Band conducted by Ray Watson. Seats are limited but there's plenty of standing space.

Another main attraction of the evening is a demonstration by the emergency services on the field beside the sports stadium. You can watch the skills of various rescue teams as they demonstrate how to save people from a burning building. Exciting stuff, so I'm told. You can buy tickets at the gates when they open at twenty hundred hours and car parking is free.

On Saturday morning, there's a children's road race for children who are ten to fourteen years old. If you want your child to enter, you must collect an entry form from the Festival office and hand it in at the start of the race. Once your child has filled in the form, make sure that they get an adult's signature – either their teacher, Mum or Dad or a neighbour – anyone so long as they're over eighteen. Everyone in the race must be in the Town Hall Square by ten on Saturday morning at the latest, as that's when the race begins. The course is two kilometres long and the roads will be closed while everyone is running. Later on in the morning there's a competition to find Bampton's best entertainer who…

P   *Now listen again.*

That is the end of Part Three. You now have a minute to check your answers. We will tell you when Part Four begins.

Now turn to Part Four, questions 20–25. Look at the six statements for this Part. You will hear a conversation over the telephone between a shopkeeper and a woman about a bill. Decide if you think each statement is correct or incorrect. If you think it is correct, put a tick in the box under A for YES. If you think it is not correct, put a tick in the box under B for NO. At the end, the recording is repeated.

Now we are ready to start. Listen carefully…

V1   Hello. 894755.
V2   Is that Mrs Enright?
V1   Yes, speaking.
V2   This is Mr Jameson from the Bed Shop.
V1   Oh hello, Mr Jameson.
V2   I'm sorry to trouble you, Mrs Enright, but I wonder if you could let us have your payment for the beds which we delivered to you two months ago. It's rather a large sum of money, as you know. They were expensive beds…
V1   But it's been paid, Mr Jameson!
V2   Um, I think you'll find that it hasn't.
V1   But I paid it myself. About a week after the beds arrived, I came into your store.
V2   And do you remember how you paid it? By cheque, was it?
V1   No, most unusually for me, I actually had enough cash with me. I had some foreign money left over from my holiday so I changed it and decided to use that. Normally I would have used my credit card.
V2   And you paid this into our accounts office?
V1   Of course! I remember the clerk being surprised at all the cash. She said she'd never had a bill paid like that before! She laughed at the fact that I had all the notes and coins in a little bag.
V2   This is very odd. The clerk doesn't remember the bill being paid and…
V1   But that's ridiculous!
V2   Well, if it was paid you'll have a receipt, so if you wouldn't

mind coming into the store and bringing that with you, I'm sure…

V1 But it's two months ago. I haven't kept the receipt. Why would I keep it once I'd paid for everything? I've been a customer of yours for years and nothing like this has ever happened before.

V2 Now please, Mrs Enright, don't upset yourself. I'm sure we can sort this out. Can I ask you to come into the shop as soon as you can? I don't want to call in the police. I'd like to sort this out personally if I can. I'll have another word with our clerk and ask our bank to look at…

P *Now listen again.*

That is the end of Part Four. You now have twelve minutes to check and transfer your answers to the answer sheet.

That is the end of the Test.

TEST 4

P *This is Preliminary Test Four. There are four Parts to the Test. You will hear each recording twice. During the Test there will be a pause before each Part to allow you to look through the questions, and other pauses to let you think about your answers. You should write your answers on the question paper. You will have twelve minutes at the end to transfer your answers to the separate answer sheet.*

Part One
There are seven questions in this Part. For each question there are four pictures and a short recording. You will hear each recording twice. For each question, look at the pictures and listen to the recording. Choose the correct picture and put a tick in the box below it.

Before we start, here is an example.

What time is the match?

V1 Are you going to watch the match on television tonight?
V2 I don't know. What time's it on?
V1 Ten past eight.

P *The woman says the match starts at ten past eight. The first picture is correct and the tick has been put in the box under the picture.*

Now we are ready to start. Here is a short recording for the first four pictures. Don't forget to put a tick in one of the boxes! Listen carefully…

One *What is the man holding?*

V1 What've you got behind your back? No, don't tell me – chocolates!
V2 No, these!
V1 Oh, they're lovely, and my favourite colour roses too! Thank you!

P **Two** *Which picture describes the fisherman's day?*

V1 Have you caught any fish yet?
V2 You bet. How about that one in the basket?
V1 Gosh, it's enormous. I hope you're going to throw it back.

P **Three** *What is happening?*

V1 Look, that little girl over there by the tree is crying.
V2 No, she isn't.
V1 She is. You can see the tears on her cheeks.

P **Four** *Who is waiting for Mr Svenson?*

V Will Mr Svenson, recently arrived from Stockholm, please come to the customer services desk where his wife and two children are waiting for him?

P **Five** *Which bed does the woman want?*

V1 Which bed would you like? They both seem very comfortable.
V2 If you don't mind, I'd like the bed with the bedside light so I can read. I've almost finished that thriller I started yesterday.
V1 That's fine by me. I'm too tired to read anyway.

P **Six** *Which book does the girl buy?*

V1 Are you buying that book on ships? I didn't know you were interested in ships!
V2 I'm not. I've just been looking at the pictures. No, this is the one I'm buying – on modern aircraft.
V1 I thought you hated flying.
V2 I do, but I love watching planes.

P **Seven** *Where does the man put the playing cards?*

V1 Where shall I put these playing cards? By the TV?
V2 No, I like to keep that table clear. Can you put them on that shelf under the plants, please.
V1 Sure.

P *That is the end of Part One. You now have half a minute to check your answers. We will tell you when Part Two begins.*

Now turn to Part Two, questions 8–13. Look at the questions for this Part.

You will hear a radio programme about traffic and travel. Put a tick in the correct box for each question. At the end, the recording is repeated.

Now we are ready to start. Listen carefully…

V1 … and now at 9.00 a.m., we come to our weekend travel check with Polly Burton.
V2 Good morning. And after a week which has been problem-free, I'm afraid there are difficulties ahead for some of you planning to travel this weekend. However, the weather forecast is for less rain, so that's something.

First of all, for those of you travelling into London. There has been a crash on the M4 motorway and police say that long queues of cars are building up. You should try to leave the motorway at exit number 3, and take another route using one of the main roads into the capital.

In the centre of London, a lorry has lost its load of bottles while crossing London Bridge. Police warn that there is a lot of broken glass not just on the road but on the pavements as well, and it will take a few hours before everything has been cleared up. If you can, you should avoid walking or driving over London Bridge until after midday.

If you are planning on travelling by train over the weekend, checking train times with your local station is essential before leaving home. There is a lot of engineering work and although most services are normal, some journeys may take longer than usual.

Now for those of you flying from Manchester airport and hoping to leave your car at the airport car park: be prepared for delays, or better still, leave your car at home. Part of the underground car park is being rebuilt at the moment so only half the usual car park spaces are in use. You may arrive to find that there is no space at all! So do try to use public transport to reach the airport.

We have also been told that university students in Birmingham are planning to march through the city centre this afternoon to protest against rent increases. This means that the main shopping streets will be closed to private traffic from noon, and police expect the march to last at least two hours. If you are planning on shopping in Birmingham city centre you may prefer to travel into the city by bus.

And finally for those of you using the M6 motorway. The motorway police are asking motorists to watch for signs telling them to reduce speed. There is thick fog on some sections of the M6 which is not likely to clear before mid-morning. It rained heavily during the night and the motorway can be dangerous if you are driving too fast and suddenly run into fog. You have been listening to…

P *Now listen again.*

That is the end of Part Two. You now have a minute to check your answers. We will tell you when Part Three begins.

Now turn to Part Three, questions 14–19. Look at the notes about recommended hotels. Some information is missing. You will hear a radio presenter talking about which hotels to stay at. For each question, fill in the missing information in the numbered space. At the end, the recording is repeated.

Now we are ready to start. Listen carefully…

V … and now we come to the part of the programme where we recommend where to stay. So have pencil and paper ready and at the end of the programme I'll give you addresses and telephone numbers. I'll also be giving fax numbers, although faxing a reservation is usually more expensive.

As we mentioned earlier, if you're looking for an hotel on the lakeside, we recommend Hotel Flora, which is beautifully situated. Each room has TV and radio, its own bathroom and prices include a buffet breakfast. Lunch and dinner cost extra but, as there are lots of eating places along the lakeside, you'll probably want to explore those. Do reserve accommodation early, however, as the hotel is very popular in the summer season.

Hotel Flora is quite expensive, so if you're looking for something a little cheaper, then try the Gold Cross Hotel. This is a family-owned business. The hotel, which was originally a small school, only has sixteen rooms but all the rooms have their own shower. Prices are for accommodation only, but there is a dining room where you can have a good breakfast at a reasonable price. As this hotel is in the centre of town, there is no parking area, although there is an underground car park not far away where you can leave a car overnight for a small fee.

If you want a really modern hotel try the Hotel Continental. This is a large luxury hotel where guests can swim in a heated pool – wait for it – on the hotel roof! It also has an excellent restaurant which is famous for its desserts. All the rooms have TV, radio, fridge and mini-bar. If you want a room with a view of the mountains then you'll be charged extra. In my opinion, though, it's worth it. You can sit on your balcony and watch the sun slip down behind…

P *Now listen again.*

That is the end of Part Three. You now have a minute to check your answers. We will tell you when Part Four begins.

Now turn to Part Four, questions 20–25. Look at the six statements for this Part. You will hear a conversation between two people who are deciding where to go for the evening. Decide if you think each statement is correct or incorrect. If you think it is correct, put a tick in the box under A for YES. If you think it is not correct, put a tick in the box under B for NO. At the end, the recording is repeated.

Now we are ready to start. Listen carefully…

V1 Hi, I'm home.

V2 Hi. Did you remember to get the tickets?

V1 Well, I remembered, but they were sold out.

V2 Oh no. I was really looking forward to it. It's the last night that play is on.

V1 I know. We should have booked last week. Anyway, I'm sure there'll be another chance to see it. The thing is, what do we do now? Shall we go out for a meal?

V2 No. We did that last weekend.

V1 What about a concert?

V2 I never see the point in paying to go to a concert. I mean you can buy tapes and CDs and listen at home or on the radio.

V1 But then you can get a video of a film, so I don't understand your argument.

V2 Yes, but you can never get the video until a long time after the film has come out. It's a waste of money going to a concert.

V1 It's not. I love seeing a live performance. There's always such a fantastic feeling in the audience, such an atmosphere.

V2 We could go and see my aunt. We said we'd call in last week and we didn't have time.

V1 I did not finish work early so that we could go and see one of your relations. How about going down to the sports centre? I could do with some exercise and…

V2 I don't feel the least bit energetic. I've had a very hard day and the last thing I want is to run around.

V1 All right. But so far you haven't suggested anything other than a family visit. I think we should stay in and watch television if we can't agree what else to do. There might be a good film on.

V2 OK. But another time, let's plan ahead and make sure we get tickets for things we want to see.

P *Now listen again.*

That is the end of Part Four. You now have twelve minutes to check and transfer your answers to the answer sheet.

That is the end of the Test.

TEST 5

P *This is Preliminary Test Five. There are four Parts to the Test. You will hear each recording twice. During the Test there will be a pause before each Part to allow you to look through the questions, and other pauses to let you think about your answers. You should write your answers on the question paper. You will have twelve minutes at the end to transfer your answers to the separate answer sheet.*

Part One
There are seven questions in this Part. For each question, there are four pictures and a short recording. You will hear each recording twice. For each question, look at the pictures and listen to the recording. Choose the correct picture and put a tick in the box below it.

Before we start, here is an example.

What time is the match?

V1 Are you going to watch the match on television tonight?

V2 I don't know. What time's it on?

V1 Ten past eight.

P *The woman says the match starts at ten past eight. The first picture is correct and the tick has been put in the box under the picture.*

Now we are ready to start. Here is a short recording for the first four pictures.

Don't forget to put a tick in one of the boxes! Listen carefully…

One *Where are they meeting?*

V1 You're in a hurry!

V2 I know, I'm late. I've got an appointment with a journalist to do an interview and I should have met him over an hour ago. He said he'd wait outside the cathedral. I just hope he's still there!

P **Two** *What are the shoes like?*

V1 I like your shoes! I've been looking for a pair like that with flat heels and round toes for ages.

V2 Well, I got these in the market. They've got plenty – you should have a look.

P **Three** *What can they see?*

V1 Look at the people in that rowing boat. I'm sure they're in trouble. One of them keeps waving and the other one is just hanging over the side.

V2 You're right. Come on, let's go and get help.

P **Four** *What is he looking for?*

V1 What're you looking for?

V2 My exercise book – the one with the snooker players on the front that I use for physics.

V1 It's over there by your walkman.

P **Five** *What's the matter?*

V1 Can you hear someone screaming?

V2 Yes, it's that baby over there. He doesn't like being left outside the newsagent's.

V1 Oh, poor thing. I'll go over and play with him then.

P **Six** *What's happening?*

V1 I'm sure that building's on fire.

V2 Don't be silly.

V1 Well, look at the smoke pouring out from under the roof. I'm going to phone the fire brigade.

P **Seven** *What's the complaint?*

V1 Who made this bed?

V2 I did.

V1 Well, you've forgotten to put the pillow back and what's all this jewellery doing on the bed?

V2 Oh, sorry. I'll tidy it away.

P *That is the end of Part One. You now have half a minute to check your answers. We will tell you when Part Two begins.*

Now turn to Part Two, questions 8–13. Look at the questions for this Part.

You will hear an announcement on board a ship. Put a tick in the correct box for each question. At the end, the recording is repeated.

Now we are ready to start. Listen carefully…

V Good morning, ladies and gentlemen. This is Bob, your entertainments officer for the day. If I could have your attention for a few minutes, I'd like to tell you what's on today's programme.

First off, for those of you who are feeling energetic, the keep fit class meets on the lower deck in twenty minutes at nine hundred hours. If you haven't been along before, why not come along and join in some gentle exercise in the ship's gym? However, for those of you feeling more energetic, this morning's jogging session will be taken by Jim and he'll be starting out from the games room on C deck at nine thirty. Please make sure you are wearing trainers and light clothes for both these activities.

This morning's talk will be given by the ship's doctor in the main dining room and begins at eleven hundred hours. It is called 'You and Your Lifestyle' and Dr Northam will be asking each of you to fill in your own personal health questionnaire at the start of the talk. This will help you and

Dr Northam to discuss various aspects of your own individual lifestyles which you might like to change or improve. It promises to be an interesting and entertaining hour.

If you missed yesterday's competitions in the swimming pool, then come along this afternoon at fifteen hundred hours for more fun and games. You don't need to be able to swim and it's one way of keeping cool as it looks set to be a really clear cloudless day, unlike yesterday, when you probably needed an extra sweater!

Now, on to this evening, and there's a change to the advertised film programme. Starting in the ship's cinema at twenty hundred hours – not twenty-one hundred as advertised – is the classic movie *The Singing Moon*. There are no tickets for this event, but as seats are rather limited, you're advised to come along early.

And then, straight after the movie, for the night owls amongst you, is the late-night disco. If you have a special record request, why not hand it in to me during the day and I'll do my best to make sure it's played at tonight's disco, which starts at twenty-three hundred hours and goes on until – well, who knows? – whenever you decide and that's late, late, late… but we'll let you go to bed before breakfast…

P *Now listen again.*

That is the end of Part Two. You now have a minute to check your answers. We will tell you when Part Three begins.

Now turn to Part Three, questions 14–19. Look at the notes about a radio competition. Some information is missing. You will hear a radio presenter talking about the competition. For each question, fill in the missing information in the numbered space. At the end, the recording is repeated.

Now we are ready to start. Listen carefully.

V … so congratulations to last week's winner, who will shortly be receiving the top twenty classical compact discs. And now on to the competition spot of the week. Make sure you've got a pen or pencil ready so you can write down the details. And make sure you're near a phone so you can ring in. Right.

This week we're offering ten prizes, so there's a chance for ten people to win two free tickets for the Laser Show at the International Football Stadium. It's absolutely brilliant so if *you* want to be there on April 23rd, all you have to do is answer three questions and then ring us on 0151 66438.

You must have all three answers before you ring in. Then you will be asked for your name and address, your telephone number and your age. The first five correct callers will each receive two tickets, so you can take a friend with you, or your mum or dad or your grandma! The usual twelve lines will be open at the end of the programme, so give us a ring as soon as you know the answers.

Please don't write in to the programme with your answers. If you can't get through the first time, then keep trying. But, and it's a big but, you can only make one call and, in order to win the two tickets, your three answers must be completely correct. OK then? Got your pencils? Good luck – and here is the first question: who said, 'If you want to…'

P *Now listen again.*

That is the end of Part Three. You now have a minute to check your answers. We will tell you when Part Four begins.

Now turn to Part Four, questions 20–25. Look at the six statements for this Part. You will hear a conversation between a woman called Tanya and a man called Bob who are walking home after a meal in a restaurant. Decide if you think each statement is correct or incorrect. If you think it is correct, put a tick in the box under A for YES. If you think it is not correct, put a tick in the box under B for NO. At the end, the recording is repeated.

Now we are ready to start. Listen carefully…

V1 I don't know about you, Tanya, but I'm still hungry.

V2 No, I'm fine. It was a good meal. Rather expensive though.

V1 More than rather! I thought they charged far too much for what we got.

V2 But if you want to eat out somewhere good, you have to be prepared to pay quite a lot. It's not just the food you're paying for. You pay for the surroundings, the service, the live music – even the fresh flowers on the table. It's all those things which make it such an enjoyable evening.

V1 I suppose so. But I think it'd be better to buy something really special and eat it at home.

V2 Oh yes! And who does the cooking?

V1 I'm always ready to help.

V2 That's not the point. I want to be able to enjoy a relaxing evening and that means eating out and…

V1 And wasting money. Just think what we could have bought if we'd stayed at home.

V2 But it's not as much fun! I loved the music.

V1 Well, I just found it embarrassing. I hated it when the violinist stood right beside me. I didn't know where to look.

V2 I know.

V1 Well, you didn't help. You kept smiling at him!

V2 Oh come on, Bob. What d'you expect? He's got to earn his living. It must be really difficult to play for people who behave as if they can't see you!

V1 Well, I was there to eat. If I wanted to go to a concert…

V2 I know, you'd have bought tickets. Well – we won't go there again. We'll try that new place next time. The service was awfully slow – we were there about four hours, you know.

V1 Now, there I *would* agree with you. That's probably why I'm hungry. It's time for the next meal!

P *Now listen again.*

That is the end of Part Four. You now have twelve minutes to check and transfer your answers to the answer sheet.

That is the end of the Test.

Sample Speaking Test

Test 1

Part 1   General conversation

Tasks Identifying oneself, giving information about people, asking direct questions.

Sub tasks Spelling, numbers, responding to questions and information.

Examiner *Hello. Please sit down.*
What are your names?
Would you tell me your candidate numbers so I can check them, please?
Do you know each other?

If *Yes* *Imagine (or pretend) that you don't know each other and find out some information about each other, please.*

If *No* *Well, I'd like you to find out some information about each other, please.*

Pause … prompt if necessary.

Candidates should contribute about four or five turns each. If necessary, prompt to elicit personal information such as home town, school or college, job or family, reasons for learning English, etc. Choose a suitable word for spelling from each candidate's contribution and ask for it at the end of the conversation, for example:

Rosa, you said you came from Avila. How do you spell that?

Pedro, you said your family name was Rodriguez. How do you spell that?

Time Allow 2–3 minutes, then at an appropriate point thank the students and move on to Part 2.

Part 2   Simulated situation

Tasks Making plans, agreeing and disagreeing, asking for and giving opinions.

Examiner [to both candidates]
I'm going to describe a situation to you.
You have been asked to organize a day trip for your English class together.
Please look at the picture on page 25.
I want you to talk about what you would like to do and what preparations you will have to make.
Just think for a few seconds.
Is that all right? Shall I repeat it?
Rosa, would you like to begin?

Allow candidates enough time to complete the task without intervening, but prompt if necessary. At an appropriate point bring the exchange to a conclusion by saying something suitable to the task, for example:
I hope you have a good day out.

Time Allow 2–3 minutes for candidates to work through the task including time to absorb the information.

Part 3   Responding to a visual stimulus

Tasks Describing people and places, saying where people are and what they are doing.

Examiner *Now I'm going to give each of you a photograph of some people. Pedro, here is your photograph.*
(Show candidate picture 1 on page 111).
Would you show it to Rosa and talk about it, please?
Rosa, I'll give you your photograph in a moment.
Right, Pedro, would you start now, please?
Thank you.

If you need to intervene, avoid direct questions but supply prompts.

Now, Rosa, here is your photograph.
(Show candidate picture 1 on page 112).
Would you show it to Pedro and tell him about it, please?
Are you ready?…
Thank you.

Allow the candidates to talk with as little intervention as possible. In talking about the pictures, they should be able to paraphrase or gloss a word in order to explain an idea if they do not know the exact word.

Remove the pictures before going on to Part 4.

Part 4   General conversation

(based on the photographs)

Tasks Talking about one's likes and dislikes, expressing opinions.

Examiner [to both candidates]
The people in your photographs were enjoying being together.
Now, I'd like you to talk to each other about spending time with friends or members of your family.
Talk about the kinds of things you like or dislike doing with your friends, and the things which you like or dislike doing with your family.

Time Allow the candidates about 5 minutes for Parts 3 and 4 together. As far as possible avoid intervening, but prompt if it is essential.

Sample student answers for Writing Part 3

The sample answers below are examples of students' work and vary in standard. After looking at the samples, teachers should refer to the mark schemes for each Test and the writing assessment criteria on page 128 in order to help them assess their own students' work.

Students are only required to transfer what they write AFTER the printed prompt. There is no need to transfer the name of the person they are writing to, but it will help them to identify with the task if they know who they are addressing in their letter.

5	very good answer at this level	
4	good answer	
3	adequate answer	
2	limited answer	
1	poor answer	
0	achieves nothing	
Total mark = task + language: maximum mark 10		

TEST 1

The answers in Test 1 reflect different levels of ability.

Sample A
Comment

This is a very good example of task fulfilment and although the language control is occasionally faulty, the student would not be penalized at this level.

Dear (Benson)

… I will meet you at the bus stop at about 11:00am on Saturday. Then I think we should have lunch first before doing anything. After lunch you could play on my TV game or we could play basketball in my garden, it should be 4.00pm by then, and I borrowed a video called "Supperman" which we can watch after dinner, which should be finished by 8:00pm, then we could go for a swim just before bed time. The next morning we could spend a whole morning watch Chinese video, and we will go to China town to go the things you want to buy before you go back to school.

Wish you good health.

> *With lots of love*
> *Tony*

Marks awarded: Task 5   Language 5

Sample B
Comment

The student has again fulfilled the task but there are more significant slips in usage which would lead to the loss of a mark for language achievement.

Dear (Carla)

… We are going to visit a very nice museum. Wait! It's a museum for young people. Then we are going to dance to a very funny disco till the morning and after having a rest we're going to visit some friends. If you want, I organized a jockey match where we can play. Appart of this, I have a friend that is very intrested in you, I hope you like him becouse is very handsome. For weekend we are going to a party in Mary's house, there you can dance, drink, listen to some National music and meet a lot of boys.

> *Love,*
> *Axel*

Marks awarded: Task 5   Language 4

Sample C
Comment

The student has misunderstood the task by referring to 'two weeks' instead of a 'weekend' and would therefore lose marks for not fulfilling the task. The language is competent and some of the vocabulary is very effective, but the short length limits the student's opportunity to gain a high mark.

Dear (Tom)

… First we will have a good dinner at home and then we'll go camping near the lake. There I would like to go swimming and fishing. We'll eat fishes and berrys. Maybe we'll go to the moiuntains and in the forest . Here we can collect wood to make a campfire and we'll roast the fishes and some sausages. We will be back two weeks later.

> *Bye*
> *Pato*

Marks awarded: Task 2   Language 3

The remaining sample answers show how students have completed the tasks at the appropriate level, even though the language is quite frequently faulty.

TEST 2

Dear (Simon)

… Our new house is in the country and is really big with a garden full of trees. I have a bedroom with my own T.V. and I can see a farm from my window. The air is much better than where I used to live, and there have many big playground, where you can play football. As there is very quiet, I can concentrate on my works which is really nice. The problems are we're new, that means we don't know our neighbours so I have got no friends to play with. But soon I should have some friends, I hope as some boys live next door. Anyway, what about you then.

From Patrick

Marks awarded: Task 5   Language 4

TEST 3

Dear (Roberto)

… How are you? I'm fine. I spent my holiday in the Europa Park with my family. I arrived on Monday and first of all we had a little rest after our long journey because we were very tired. We were very pleased to see lots of exciting things to do. On Wednesday we spent a day on the lake and we took some pack luches with us. We were in a boat and it was really fun. On Thursday we went for a walk and watched a film in the evening. It was really good. I wish I could watch it again. On Friday there was a tennis competition and the winner will have £100 and at last I won. I think I should stop now.

From
Anna

Marks awarded: Task 5   Language 4

TEST 4

Dear (Juan)

… We are staying in a house by the seaside and enjoying it. We go every day for walks in the nature. But I broke my foot while I was playing football and I was in hospital for two days and it spoild my holiday. The only thing I could do was setting

in the room and watching on the TV and soon I've fed up with it. I was left in the room by myself when everyone were playing outside which really does upset me. But now I've used to it and I did write my letters and cards. I hope you will write to me soon.

From
Marco

Marks awarded: Task 5   Language 3

TEST 5

Dear (Marta)

… Thank you very much for leting me stay at your home, I had a wonderful time during thoes days, especially the party on Friday night. It was the best I ever had and the music was wonderful too. I wish I could do the same when you stay with me. I also liked the shopping and the video we watched. You taught me quite a lot of English and my English has improved quite a lot. Please thank your parents, they had been very kind to me. Anyway thank you very much indeed.

From,
Giuliana

Marks awarded: Task 5   Language 5

	Writing assessment criteria for Part 3	
MARK	**TASK**	**LANGUAGE**
5	Very good attempt at task, covering all content elements fully, with minimal digression. Generally coherent, requiring no effort by the reader.	Generally good control, and confident use of language. Coherent linking of sentences using simple cohesive devices. Language ambitious, including complex sentences and range of structures and vocabulary. Language errors may still be present, but they are minor, due to ambition, and non-impeding.
4	Good attempt at task, covering all the content elements, with some elaboration. There may be some minor repetition or digression, though overall script is reasonably coherent and requires minimal effort by the reader.	Reasonable control of language and linking of sentences. Either language is sound but unambitious, or language ambitious, i.e. showing evidence of range of structures and vocabulary with some errors, but these generally non-impeding.
3	Reasonable attempt to cover task. May be a rather simple account with little elaboration, or a fuller attempt containing some repetition or digression. One content element may have been omitted. Coherent enough to make meaning clear, although little effort may be required by the reader.	Evidence of some control of language, and simple sentence structure generally sound. Language likely to be unambitious, or if ambitious probably flawed. A number of errors may be present, e.g. in structures, tenses, spelling, articles, prepositions, but they are generally non-impeding. Linking of sentences not always maintained.
2	Some attempt at task, possibly with limited understanding. Two content elements may have been omitted, or there will be noticeable irrelevance or incoherence, which will require considerable effort by the reader. Task may be unfinished.	Erratic control of sentence structure and use of tenses, e.g. past simple not used appropriately in many cases. Language may be very simplistic/limited/repetitive. Errors in the spelling of PET vocabulary often occur. Language errors will impede communication at times. Punctuation may be noticeably absent, leading to incoherence of sentences.
1	Poor attempt at task, because has little relevance, is far too short or very incoherent.	Very poor control of language. Difficult to understand due to, e.g. frequent grammatical errors, errors in spelling of PET level words, or poor sentence construction. There may be a general absence of punctuation, leading to serious incoherence.
0	Candidate has misunderstood or misinterpreted task. Content bears no relation to task.	Achieves nothing, language impossible to understand.

NB These guidelines are subject to amendment.

207379